MODERN
ORGANIZATION

MODERN ORGANIZATION

VICTOR·A·THOMPSON

SECOND EDITION

THE UNIVERSITY OF ALABAMA PRESS

Tuscaloosa and London

THIRD PRINTING

First edition copyright © 1961
by Victor A. Thompson
Second edition copyright © 1977
by Victor A. Thompson

First edition published 1961
by Random House, Inc.
Reprinted 1963, 1964, 1965, 1966,
1967, 1968

Second edition published 1977
by The University of Alabama Press

Library of Congress Cataloging in Publication Data

Thompson, Victor Alexander.
Modern organization.

Bibliography: p.
Includes index.
1. Organization.   2.   Bureaucracy.   I.   Title.
HD31.T49   1977   658   77-6664
ISBN 0-8173-4838-7

FOR

Nora, Vicki, and Sandy

PREFACE

꩜

MODERN ORGANIZATION was inspired by the desire to reconcile the received traditions in administration with the new perspectives, theories, and research findings of sociology and social psychology. Its major theme is the clash between authority on the one hand, and growing information and knowledge on the other. This clash has resulted in a central and persistent dilemma for modern administration—the right to command *versus* the knowledge to do wisely.

Among the most crucial problems of the modern world is how to bring knowledge and power together. At the level of society as a whole, there has been strong temptation and pressure and some movement to reduce the power of democratic institutions like parties and legislatures and to increase the power of institutions perceived to be more knowledgeable and expert, especially administrative organizations. From some academic quarters come proposals urging administrators to take over functions which have traditionally belonged to legislatures, boards of directors, and the like. Business managers are pressured to seek goals other than the economic interests of their shareholders (the owners of their organizations); and public managers are urged to pursue various conceptions of morality and virtue regardless of directions from apathetic majorities and their representatives.

Within organizations, the solution to the problem of bringing knowledge and power together is predominantly sought through the staff system. As the First Hoover Commission on reorganization of the federal administration said: "The wise exercise of authority is impossible without the aids which staff institutions can provide. . . ." The great authority of position given to mortal human beings within our administrative organizations is typically informed by surrounding it with a number of specialized "staff assistants." The authority of the position, combined with the knowledge of staff specialists, may produce centers of great power. But it also produces a new problem—whose power is it? Within administrative circles it is customary to put this problem out of sight by pretending that staff assistants are merely extensions of the executive who occupies the position of authority; that the power created by combining positional authority with specialized staff knowledge is the power of that executive; and that he is held accountable for its use by representatives of the owners, such as a board of directors or a legislative committee. However, when a bureaucracy is created to control and direct another bureaucracy, the question remains: who controls the first bureaucracy (the staff)? If the executive did not have the knowledge to control and direct the one, he will not have the knowledge to control and direct the other. Since this book was first written, Watergate has provided a dramatic if painful example of how the staff system can create centers of irresponsible power.

Some people approach the problem of bringing knowledge and authority together by falling back on childhood phantasies and seeking a father substitute (perhaps now a mother substitute). They seek an all-knowledgeable and impeccably virtuous administrator to whom our awe-inspiring array of problems can be turned over. They urge administrative or executive training programs and curricula to turn out executives who have mastered all relevant fields of knowledge—who are "generalists" rather than specialists. A little thought will disclose all such proposals to be essentially regressive—a search for a hero or a magic helper. The problem of authority with knowledge will not be solved thus. It will be solved, if at all, by hard and careful administrative analysis, thinking, and programming—by devising administrative arrangements and procedures for bringing knowledge to bear on problems and motivating specialized, and hence informed, employees of organizations to participate faithfully in these arrangements and procedures.

The prerequisite for successfully devising such arrangements is more information about the nature of modern complex organizations. This book is intended as a contribution to the growing understanding of organizations. It focuses on the general aspects of modern organizations, those which many of them share, rather than pointing up and explaining differences. A good deal of organization research, especially that oriented to the discovery and explanation of variations, takes the major part of the organization for granted. For example, studies of the relation between leadership styles and output compare the behavior of superiors toward subordinates and meticulously classify small variations in this behavior while overlooking the enormous institutional fact that we have superiors and subordinates in the first place. It is like studying the tip of the iceberg and ignoring the submerged ninety percent. This book is oriented toward the neglected ninety percent. Of course, this ninety percent is not submerged. In fact, it is so much out in the open that it is not seen. It is simply taken for granted. Both perspectives are needed—the careful observation and explanation of small behavioral variations and the more holistic institutional approach of this book. Furthermore, the latter must come before the analysis of behavioral variations if studies of this kind are to have value. The book apparently has been successful in finding this general level of description and explanation because it has been used as much in Colleges of Business Administration and other centers of administrative studies as it has been in public administration education and training. This inexpensive paperback edition will make it possible to continue that tradition.

VICTOR A. THOMPSON

Gainesville, Florida
February, 1977

CONTENTS

MODERN
ORGANIZATION

CHAPTER 1

Introduction

🎜

1. *Thesis*

CURRENT INTEREST in problems of organization reflects the great extent to which modern man's life is organized for him. His education, his livelihood, his recreation, and even his religion are products of the planned and co-ordinated activities of great numbers of people most of whom he has never met and never will. He is a product of modern organization. His fate is vitally affected by his understanding of it. The purpose of this book is to describe and to explain organization in modern society.

Unspecialized primitive man was organized in kinship groups—family groups which served all of his needs. Such organization was inadequate for specialized man, and new forms developed. In the highly specialized industrial society of today, the predominant form of organization is a highly rationalized and impersonal integration of a large number of specialists co-operating to achieve some announced specific objective.

Superimposed upon the highly elaborated division of

work in such organizations is an also highly elaborated hierarchy of authority. We propose, following Max Weber, to call this form of organization "bureaucracy." [1] Examples would be governmental departments and business corporations. There are many nonbureaucratic kinds of organization—for example, families, clubs, political parties, associations, interest groups, churches, and schools. As some of these break away from tradition, however, rationalize their activities, divide their work on the basis of specialized, expert knowledge and ability, they become more bureaucratic. Thus, educational organizations and even some religious ones are showing signs of bureaucratization.

As the bureaucratic form has developed, associated as it is with the advance of specialization, the most stubborn problem has proved to be the securing of co-operation among individual specialists. If the problem of co-operation can be solved, it seems that specialization is capable of accomplishing almost any material objective. Increasingly large amounts of time, effort, and thought are expended on the securing of co-operation.

Today in the highly specialized societies of the West most people spend much of their time as small cogs in the machinery of large impersonal bureaucracies. It is through these structures that they must find success, that they must find their livelihood. The demands of bureaucracy govern them during most of their waking moments. The influence of bureaucracy is felt in nearly all aspects of life.

Being a cog in such machinery, the individual has lost much of the control over his own destiny. Many people have a feeling of powerlessness, of alienation, and they respond with various kinds of behavior. Some are able to manipulate organization sufficiently well to achieve important aims of their own. Others submit to bureaucratic standards of achievement and find bureaucracy a natural and comfortable habitat. Whatever the form of adjustment, behavior patterns and character types emerge which are bureaucratically con-

[1] Max Weber: *The Theory of Social and Economic Organization*, trans. A. M. Henderson and Talcott Parsons, ed. Talcott Parsons (New York: Oxford University Press, Inc.; 1947).

ditioned to some important extent. Modern man is becoming a bureaucratic man, or, as he has been called, an "Organization Man." A new ethic of co-operation begins to replace the older one of self-reliance.[2] A new management technology appears which is concerned with the recalcitrance of people, rather than with the hardness of materials.[3]

These changes have not escaped criticism from those who look nostalgically back to an earlier age.[4] In general, critics deplore the subordination of the individual to the group, "over-conformism," the derogation of individual brilliance and invention, the affectation of good will and good feeling, the devaluation of technical competence as compared to merely "getting along," the insistence on avoiding conflict. They deplore the loss of individual freedom and initiative. They deplore the bureaucratization of society.

Modern bureaucracy is an adaptation of older organizational forms, altered to meet the needs of specialization. Modern specialization is grafted onto it, but old traces of the past remain. Along with technological specialization we find survivals of Genghis Khan and aboriginal war chiefs. We find the latest in science and technology associated with the autocratic, monistic, hierarchical organization of a simpler time. We find, in short, specialization and hierarchy together.

Our analysis will revolve around the relationships between specialist and hierarchical roles. Roles, not jobs or individuals, are the basic units of analysis. For example, we will not be concerned with the "executive" as such, but with the roles he fills. Many executives perform both specialist and hierarchical roles. With increasing specialization, however,

[2] See William H. Whyte, Jr.: *The Organization Man* (New York: Simon and Schuster, Inc.; 1956). References throughout this book, however, will be to the paperback edition (Garden City, New York: Doubleday & Company, Inc.; 1957). He calls this new phenomenon the "Social Ethic."

[3] The expression is from David Riesman, Nathan Glazer, and Reuel Denney: *The Lonely Crowd* (New Haven: Yale University Press; 1950). References throughout this book, however, will be to the abridged paperback edition (Garden City, New York: Doubleday & Company, Inc.; 1953), p. 135.

[4] See Whyte: op. cit.

executives lose more and more of their specialist activities to
other specialists. At the upper reaches of large bureaucracies
the executive job and the hierarchical role become almost
synonymous, and as specialization advances they undoubtedly will become completely so.

We have said that modern bureaucracy attempts to fit
specialization into the older hierarchical framework. The fitting is more and more difficult. There is a growing gap between the right to decide, which is authority, and the power
to do, which is specialized ability. This gap is growing because technological change, with resulting increase in specialization, occurs at a faster rate than the change in cultural
definitions of hierarchical roles. This situation produces tensions and strains the willingness to co-operate. Much bureaucratic behavior can be understood as a reaction to these
tensions. In short, *the most symptomatic characteristic of
modern bureaucracy is the growing imbalance between ability and authority*. Such is our thesis.

2. A Note on Method

Although we intend to use relevant experimental findings of
laboratory research, we disclaim any intention of seeking in
this way a spurious empirical validity for our argument. We
realize that copious reference to laboratory experiments is
often so used. Many of these experimental findings are of
doubtful value to real life, involving, as the experiments
often do, contrived situations with small groups of students
or children. It is sad, but very often in social science what
can be quantified is trivial. It would be foolish, however, to
overlook this experimental material, and such will be presented as suggestive rather than conclusive.

Some students of organization attempt to base their
study of the subject upon a consideration of how individuals
within organizations decide to do what they do. This orientation gives rise to the currently popular "decision-making"
approach. The basic tool of this approach is an individualis-

tic psychology. Although "decision-making" theory has undoubtedly made valuable contributions to the understanding of organizations, we believe its usefulness for our purpose is very limited. An organization is not merely the chance result of a number of decisions made by a number of rational decision makers. Only decisions of decision makers already *in* the organization, and only their *organizational* decisions, are relevant. The organization, therefore, must first be accounted for, or decision-making theory never gets beyond individual psychology.

The choice mechanism operates on those elements in the situation which are not handed down or given in advance. The elements which are given in advance are not subject to choice. They constitute the *structure* of the decisional situation. They are the environmental conditions of choice. They give order to choice. Without referring to these given elements we could not explain order, and we could not predict. When we have specified these given elements in an organizational situation, we have described the organization. We have also explained the system of order which is the organization. Looked at from this point of view, the study of decision making and the study of organization appear as theoretically separate fields. An organization is a particular kind of ordering of human behavior. The task of organization theory is to describe and explain this particular kind of order.

The decision-making approach, with its individualistic psychology, tends to hide the institutional bases of events, the structure of the situations within which decisions occur, and consequently the structural determinants of action. For this reason it tends to be ideological; it tends to protect and to preserve the institutional status quo. Our basic approach, on the contrary, will be sociological. It will concentrate on the structural determinants of behavior and will attempt to analyze behavior functionally.

As used here, "structure" refers to the persistent qualities or given elements in the environmental conditions of choice or action which make it possible to explain and perhaps to predict action. Once we understand the structure of the decisional situation, the action followed by the deciding person becomes logically understandable.

By "function" is meant the practical result produced by an action, relationship, event (or a combination of them) in relation to some value or group of values. People and groups have purposes; activities have functions. Whether the purpose is achieved or not, the act will have functions. Behavior may be functional with regard to one set of values, may preserve or promote them, but dysfunctional with regard to another. The principal focus of our functional analysis will be two-fold: first, the formal, objective, external goal of the organization; and secondly, the personal goals which participants hope to achieve by associating with the organization. That is to say, we shall be interested in the impact of various organizational activities and relationships upon these two sets of values.[5]

One final point needs to be made. Organization theory is not concerned with personality. Personality theory attempts to account for variations in individual behavior. Organization theory attempts to account for order in behavior. A bureaucratic organization is a structure composed of authority, status, technical, and social relationships. This structure can tolerate considerable variation in personalities. Organization theory, therefore, assumes a very general standard personality. Not all behavior of persons in organizations can be explained by organization theory; some will have to be referred to psychological and psychoanalytic techniques and categories of explanation; some will yield only to physical, physiological, or even chemical techniques of explanation. A full account of the behavior of people sitting at their desks would include the laws of gravity, the chemistry of desk and

[5] On the structural-functional approach see Talcott Parsons: "The Present Position and Prospects of Systematic Theory in Sociology," in George Gurvitch and Wilbert E. Moore, eds.: *Twentieth Century Sociology* (New York: Philosophical Library, Inc.; 1945). See also Robert K. Merton: "Manifest and Latent Functions," in *Social Theory and Social Structure*, rev. ed. (Glencoe, Illinois: The Free Press; 1957), pp. 19-84.

chair, the physiology of the people sitting there, and many other considerations, including temperature and the time of day. Organization theory is only concerned with those aspects of behavior which are determined by organizational structures.

This exclusion of personality from our account may seem wrong to many persons in supervisory positions. Many may feel that most of their problems stem from individual idiosyncrasies. They feel this way because they take the organization for granted. The few "personality cases" are easy to see, and they take up time. The enormous system of order, the organization, goes unnoticed. The deviant is a "personality problem" precisely because he does not respond to organizational determinants; his behavior cannot be explained by organization theory and must be referred to personality theory. Fortunately, the very general standard personality assumed by organization theory fits most people, otherwise, organizations would have to be managed from top to bottom by psychiatrists.

There is undoubtedly some interplay between personality and organization structure. This subject has received little systematic attention as of yet. To explore it will require a theory of organization somewhat more completely worked out than we have had up to the present time. It is our hope that this book will make some contribution toward the development of such a theory.

CHAPTER 2

Bureaucracy

☘

1. Max Weber and the Theory of Bureaucracy

THE GREAT German sociologist, Max Weber, was the first to
attempt a systematic theory of bureaucratic organization.
His views remain important to us not only because of his
enormous influence on American social scientists, but also because of the continuing validity of much of his analysis.

Weber pictured an evolution of organizational forms in
terms of the kind of authority relations within them.[1] At one
extreme is a simple, relatively nonspecialized kind of organization in which followers give almost unqualified obedience
to a leader endowed with "charisma"—presumed unusual,
generally magical powers. Such organization was primitive
in the sense that it was based upon belief in magic. Since
their prerogatives depended upon their leader's charisma, his
immediate staff felt insecure and sought a firmer legitimation of these prerogatives. Their fears came to a head at the

[1] Max Weber: *The Theory of Social and Economic Organization*,
trans. A. M. Henderson and Talcott Parsons, ed. Talcott Parsons (New
York: Oxford University Press, Inc.; 1947).

time of succession in the leadership. Routinization of methods used to obtain a successor and thus to secure staff prerogatives resulted in the traditionalistic form of organization. Monarchy would be an example.[2]

Weber conceived of the world as becoming progressively rationalized and demystified, with corresponding change in organizational forms. Both charismatic and traditional authority become harder to maintain, and a new, rationalized, legalistic kind of authority and structure emerged. He called this kind of organization "bureaucracy."

Weber believed in a cycle of change from charismatic to traditionalistic and bureaucratic forms of organization against a background of increasing rationalization. Charisma disrupts and is antithetical to the process of rationalization. Charismatic leadership is needed when existing routines cannot cope with growing problems or crises. The charismatic personality emerges and overshadows routine and procedure.[3]

Weber specified a list of criteria for the fully developed bureaucratic form, including technical training of officials, merit appointments, fixed salaries and pensions, assured careers, the separation of organizational rights and duties from the private life of the employee, and a fixed and definite division of work into distinct offices or jobs. He noted that all offices were arranged in a clear hierarchy of subordination and superordination, that members of the organization were subject to strict and systematic control and discipline, and that a rationalized set of rules and regulations tied the whole organization together. He said that it should make no difference how these rules and regulations were adopted, whether they were autocratically imposed or adopted by consent. He also said that obedience to commands should be prompt, automatic, unquestioning.

He noted that the principal general social consequences of this organizational form were a tendency toward social leveling, resulting from the attempt to get the broadest possible basis for recruitment of technical competence; a tendency

[2] See Alvin W. Gouldner: *Studies in Leadership: Leadership and Democratic Action* (New York: Harper & Brothers; 1950), p. 645.
[3] Ibid.

toward plutocracy, resulting from an interest in the greatest possible length of technical training; and the dominance of a spirit of formalistic impersonality, resulting in the minimization of hatred, of affection, and of enthusiasm.

He felt that the superiority over other forms of organization lay in its capacity to command and to utilize technical knowledge; or as we would say, in specialization. "The choice is only that between bureaucracy and dilettantism in the field of administration." [4]

2. *Some Characteristics of Modern Bureaucracy*

Although Weber sought to explain bureaucracy by means of a perhaps dubious historical law of increasing rationality,[5] his description of bureaucratic organization seems, in effect, to be consistent with our own.[6] Modern organization has evolved from earlier forms by incorporating advancing specialization. In an earlier period organizations could depend much more on the "line of command." The superior could

[4] Ibid., p. 336.

[5] See Carl J. Friedrich: "Some Observations on Weber's Analysis of Bureaucracy," in Robert K. Merton, *et al.*, eds.: *Reader in Bureaucracy* (Glencoe, Illinois: The Free Press; 1952), pp. 27-33. Although Weber characterized his depiction of bureaucracy as an "ideal type," Friedrich argues that it is neither typical nor ideal but based on impressions, particularly impressions of the Prussian bureaucracy of his time. See also Hans H. Gerth and C. Wright Mills: "A Marx for the Managers," in Merton, *et al.*: op. cit., pp. 165-78.

[6] For a nonhistorical, noncultural explanation of modern organization, see James G. March and Herbert A. Simon: *Organizations* (New York: John Wiley & Sons, Inc.; 1958), ch. vi. They suggest that organization arises out of the limitations on human rational capacities. Chester Barnard said that organizations arise out of man's biological limitations in general: *The Functions of the Executive* (Cambridge: Harvard University Press; 1938). One can hardly disagree with these views. If we did not need organizations, we would not have them. The important question, however, is why organization takes the specific form it does. This is a question which cannot be answered without reference to history and culture, any more than a particular language can be deduced from human nature.

tell others what to do because he could master the knowledge and techniques necessary to do so intelligently. As science and technology developed, the superior lost to experts the *ability* to command in one field after another, but he retained the *right* as part of his role.

A great structure of specialized competencies has grown up around the chain of command. Organizations have grown in size because they must be able fully to employ the new specialists and the specialized equipment associated with them if the organizations are to meet their competition. As more specialists appear and the organization continues to grow in size, it becomes necessary to group employees into units, and the units into larger units. Some of the larger of these units in government have been called "bureaus," and so the kind of organization resulting from this process has been called "bureaucracy." (These units were called "bureaus" from the French word for writing table or desk.)

The impact of specialization upon modern organization accounts for many of the latter's characteristic features. Because the modern organization evolves in response to modern science and technology, it reflects the guiding spirit of science and technology. This is the spirit of *rationalism*.[7] No longer are traditional or religious standards to be the guardians of knowledge. The quest for truth is to be limited and guided only by reason and empirical verification. Within the modern bureaucratic organization this rationalism expresses itself in constant self-scrutiny. The pragmatic test grows in importance. "How does it promote the organizational goal?" is the question most often heard. Although other evaluative criteria can be observed in modern bureaucracy, the pragmatic test seems to have become institutionalized. By this we mean that people seem to feel that they ought to apply that test to all arrangements.

The growing dominance of the spirit of rationalism in modern bureaucracy simply reflects the growing influence of scientific and technical specialists upon organizational de-

---

[7] We are using the term "rationalism" and its various derivatives according to common usage—not in its philosophically technical sense as an antiempirical theory of knowledge.

cisions. The bureaucratic organization is the arena where science and technology are applied. With a few rapidly disappearing exceptions, such as medicine, we can say that the application and development of science and technology depend upon bureaucratic organization. As a consequence of the dominance of this spirit of rationalism and the influence of specialists on decisions, modern bureaucratic organization is the most productive arrangement of human effort that man has thus far contrived. Its ability to accomplish objective organizational goals has produced the highest standard of living yet achieved by man, while allowing populations to expand enormously at the same time. Not only has the poverty of the industrial worker been eliminated, but, as we shall see later, the industrial laborer is becoming a technically trained specialist.

Dependence upon highly trained specialists requires *appointment by merit* rather than election or political appointment. It requires *a system of assured careers;* otherwise, the individual would not invest the time needed to acquire specialized skill. It requires that the organization have a definite and reasonably assured division of work into defined jobs or offices. The trained specialist would not usually allow himself to be used as a jack-of-all-trades. In fact, the division of work in organizations for the most part simply follows the existing specializations in society at large.

As Weber said, charismatic forms of organization give way to bureaucracy because the former are inadequate for daily, regularized activity. Charisma functions in new situations and is not compatible with highly defined situations. Charismatic organization is dependent upon the reputed genius of individuals and is, therefore, unstable and precarious. To secure stability, continuity, and predictability of product, the activities of the organization are reduced to procedures or routines. *Routinization of organizational activity* is implicit in the process of specialization and is a characteristic of bureaucracy. Specialization requires a stable environment and a guarantee of continuity of function. Within the organization, the specialist must practice his specialty—a group of related routines.[8] Although managerial ideology still strongly contains the charismatic image, bureaucratic organizations seek to avoid dependence upon individuals by reducing relevant information to classes, and organizational activity to routines which are activated when the appropriate class of information is perceived.[9] It would seem, therefore, that the advance of specialization requires routinization, one of the central characteristics of bureaucratic organization.

Organizations as problem-solving mechanisms depend upon a *factoring of the general goal into subgoals* and these into sub-subgoals, and so on, until concrete routines are reached. These subgoals are allocated to organizational units and become the goals of those units. Individuals in the units are not given the impossible task, therefore, of evaluating their every action in terms of the general goal of the organization, but only in terms of the particular subgoal allocated to their unit. The definition of the situation is sufficiently simplified to bring it within the rational capacity of the human mind. If the factoring is accurate, rationality in terms of each unit will be rationality in terms of the organization as a whole. In this way, bureaucratic organizations achieve rationality far beyond the capacity of any individual.

In addition to accurate factoring, rationality in terms of the whole organization requires that individuals in the subunits accept their assigned subgoal as the end or objective of

[8] Reinhard Bendix defines bureaucratization as routinization. See his *Work and Authority in Industry* (New York: John Wiley & Sons, Inc.; 1956), ch. iv.

[9] See March and Simon: op. cit., *passim*. Alfred Krupp, the German industrialist, remarked: "What I shall attempt to bring about is that nothing shall be dependent upon the life or existence of any particular person; that nothing of any importance shall happen or be caused to happen without the foreknowledge and approval of the management; that the past and determinate future of the establishment can be learned in the files of the management without asking a question of any mortal." See Frederick J. Nussbaum: *A History of the Economic Institutions of Modern Europe* (New York: F. S. Crofts & Co., Inc.; 1933), p. 379. Quoted in Gouldner: op. cit., pp. 179-80.

their activities. It must be the principal given value. Normally, individuals accept the assignment, since they accept the authority of the organization. Various forces, in addition, reinforce this identification with subgoals, particularly the fact that communication within the unit, and between it and the rest of the organization is heavily concerned with the subgoal. Looked at from our point of view, factoring of the organizational goal is simply differentiation of function—namely, specialization. People are to be concerned with a certain area of activities, not with all activities. Thus, specialization results in strong attachment to subgoals.

From a point of view outside a particular unit, the unit's goal is seen not as a goal, but as a means to a larger goal. From this external vantage point, therefore, the members of a unit seem to be attached to means rather than ends. One of the characteristics of bureaucratic organization based on specialization, consequently, is an *apparent inversion of ends and means*. For example, people outside a budget office frequently accuse budget officers of believing the organization exists for the purpose of operating budget procedures. From the point of view of a client interested in the general organizational goal, members of all subunits appear to have inverted means into ends. Such "inversion" may be a problem of factoring, of dividing up the work; and any necessary corrections may not be in the direction of reducing subgoal identification but, rather, of reorganization.

A *formalistic impersonality* is a readily discernible characteristic of modern organization. In interpersonal relationships, total involvement probably never occurs. Each person is concerned with somewhat less than all of the actual or potential needs of the other. In specialist relationships, involvement is limited to the needs for which the specialized function is relevant. The relationship is partial, and functional; it is "secondary" rather than "primary." The specialist performs his function for many, and so he must limit his participation in the relationship to the area of his specialty. The resulting "impersonal" relationship need not be cold or painful. When both sides recognize their mutual interdependence—the client's dependence on the specialist for the fulfillment of some need, and the specialist's dependence on the client for the opportunity to work at his calling—the relationship is not necessarily without human warmth and mutual appreciation. Pleasant though impersonal relationships of mutual interdependence abound in everyday life—the motorist and the mechanic, the doctor and the patient, the householder and the postman. Impersonality is inevitably associated with bureaucratic organization, resting as it does on specialization.

An organization based on specialization must allow specialists to practice their specialties, to carry out the routines of which their specialties are composed. Specialists do not improvise for each unique event. Improvisation is charismatic, "dilettantish." Although there are unique aspects to all events, it is only to the repeated aspects that the routines of the specialty can be applied. Consequently, specialization requires that the raw data of reality be organized into classes or categories that often recur. Furthermore, enormous amounts of information needed in a specialized world can be summarized and communicated quickly by *categorization of data*, thereby greatly facilitating the solution of problems. Therefore, although an individual is to himself a total, complete person, in some ways unique, to the specialist he is a carrier of a class of data relevant to the practice of the specialty in question. He is a speeder, an income-tax evader, a disciplinary case, an applicant for a job, a coronary, etc. The reality of the specialist is created by his classes and categories. We are all specialists in some sense, so that the realities we perceive vary from person to person. In fact, language itself is a system of categories by which we organize the raw sensory data of experience. There would appear to be no basis, therefore, for criticizing bureaucratic organizations merely because they interpret reality through specialist categories and classes. What may be important, however, is to ensure through organization that differing conceptions of reality have ample opportunity to be heard and are not simply buried under an official reality.

Bureaucratic *classification of persons* for differential treatment is reinforced by the confusion in our culture between the norm of "evenhanded" justice, on the one hand, and on the other, the ideal conception of justice as giving to each man his due. People want equality before the law in general, but individualized treatment in particular. The grouping of individuals into classes is an attempt to come closer to ideal justice without losing equality before the law. Clientele behavior enforces classification. If one individual is treated out of class, many persons who feel similarly situated will insist on equal treatment. If they are denied, it is called "discrimination." This reaction shows that these classes do exist subjectively in the particular society. Frequently this process results in the creation of new classes. Elaboration of the system of client classification approaches the ideal of individual justice. Whether one's function is regulation or service, he disregards this social process of classification at his peril.[1]

A final aspect of bureaucratic organizations, and one which often comes under criticism, is their *seeming slowness to act or to change*. In discussing this topic we must concede at the outset that bureaucratic organizations, in the face of emergencies, do often act with tremendous speed. A serious note is received from Russia, let us say, in the morning, and a reply with warlike implications is dispatched in the afternoon. A rush order is received, and all regular procedures are tacitly suspended, protocol is forgotten, and a busy, happy, problem-solving atmosphere pervades the organization until the order is out. Later in this book we shall consider this aspect of bureaucratic behavior. Here we shall point out merely that crisis situations, since they are by definition ones for which routines are not available, evoke a nonroutinized approach—a charismatic rather than a bureaucratic approach.

Under more normal conditions, organizations based upon specialization and its routines cannot be expected to react immediately to each stimulus. Great amounts of information must be accumulated if knowledge is to be substituted for

[1] For an extended discussion of the problems and processes of client classification, see Victor A. Thompson: *The Regulatory Process in OPA Rationing* (New York: King's Crown Press; 1950), pp. 122-30.

impulse, thus assuring greater effectiveness of action and greater chance of success. Since action involves many interdependent specialists, co-ordination time must be expended. In order that all necessary parts of the organization act in co-ordinated fashion, clearances must be obtained, meetings held, many copies of proposals and information memoranda prepared and properly routed. In short, if the organization could act with the speed of an individual, the organization would not be needed.

With regard to *resistance to change*, it should be noted that this phenomenon is not uniquely related to bureaucratic organizations but is a characteristic of all institutions— hence the term "cultural lag." In the case of the bureaucratic organization, however, there is special need for caution with regard to change. As we have said before, specialization requires some guarantee of stability. Specialties must not soon go out of date, or people would not invest the time needed to acquire them.

Furthermore, the members of an organization become socially specialized. They become specialized in working with one another. It takes time to convert a number of abstract, related positions into a flesh-and-blood working organization. Consequently, any suggestion for change must be measured against its effect on the co-operative system as a whole. Bureaucratic organizations must plan and control changes. Although the persons urging change may feel that the resistances they encounter represent "bureaucratic" stubbornness, the desirability of any particular change, all things considered, is usually an open question.

Internally, the bureaucratic organization is a complex structure of technical interdependence superimposed upon a strict hierarchy of authority. The entire structure is characterized by a *preoccupation with the monistic ideal*. The hierarchical institution is monocratic. It is a system of superior and subordinate role-relationships in which the superior is the *only* source of legitimate influence upon the subordinate. Everyone in the organization finds himself in such a relationship. Since this was the original organizational relationship, it has dominated organizational theory and practice and still does so. This exclusive emphasis on hierarchy has produced our prevailing organizational theory and informed management practice. We shall refer to this theory as the monistic or monocratic conception of organization. Although conditions are undoubtedly changing, it is our prevailing organizational ideal. It is well illustrated by the following quotations from the first Hoover Commission report:

> The line of command and supervision from the President down through his department heads to every employee, and the line of responsibility from each employee . . . up to the President has been weakened, or actually broken, in many places and in many ways. . . . On some occasions the responsibility of an official to his superior is obscured by laws which require him, before acting, to clear his proposals with others. This breaks the line of responsibility. . . .
> Under the President, the heads of departments must hold full responsibility for the conduct of their departments. There must be a clear line of authority reaching down through every step of the organization and no subordinate should have authority independent from that of his superior." [2]

Under the influence of the primitive monistic ideal, modern organizations are modeled more on the parent-child relationship than on the adult relationships of specialist equals and colleagues. Attempts to maintain the legitimacy of the ideal lead to a great deal of hypocrisy and pretense and to the creation of myths, such as "the ignorance of the masses," "the indispensability of leadership," and "the magical power of fear." [3] Since a monocratic institution cannot admit the

[2] Commission on Organization of the Executive Branch of the Government: *General Management of the Executive Branch* (Washington, D.C.: Government Printing Office; 1949), pp. 3-4, 34.

[3] Peter Blau: *The Dynamics of Bureaucracy* (Chicago: University of Chicago Press; 1955), p. 219.

legitimacy of conflicts, the legitimacy of divergent goals and interests, much effort is spent securing the appearance of consensus and agreement—securing a "smooth-running organization." The modern organization wants converts as much as it wants workers. It is concerned with the thoughts of its members as well as their actions, and with the thoughts of its public about the thoughts and actions of its members. Consequently, it is concerned with its members' total lives, with what they think and do away from work as well as at work.

Preoccupation with hierarchy governs the distribution of rewards by modern organizations. Ranks of deference correspond to ranks of authority, and deference is manifested by the bestowal of good things. Success within our society means, for the most part, progression up an organizational hierarchy. Modern organizations, consequently, face a growing problem of rewarding specialists. To be socially regarded as successful, specialists must give up their technical fields and enter a hierarchy. Many do, leaving us with growing shortages of many kinds of technically trained people. A few entrepreneurial specialists, such as medical doctors, have been able to avoid this dilemma, but the advance of specialization will force them all into organizations eventually—in the case of medical doctors because specialized equipment will be too costly for an individual to own, and because the health of the patient will require the co-ordinated services of many specialists.

3. *Public versus Private Bureaucracy*

Whether the organization be public or private, the configurations of bureaucracy are sufficiently the same as to enable us to discuss them together in our analysis. There will still be some who object to this point of view. They will point to the alleged "inefficiency" of public organizations, and they will attribute different motivations to public and private officials.

The growth in size and capital requirements of modern industry has resulted in the separation of ownership and management. The people who run modern business corporations are professional salaried managers.[4] Since their remuneration is not measured directly by the earnings of the corporations, it can hardly be said that their motivation is profit.[5] With the growth in size of enterprises and the professionalization of management go bureaucratic patterns of organization and management, and bureaucratic motivations.[6] Prestige, status, personal position, reduction of uncertainty, maintenance of the system of co-operation and the equilibrium of the organization—all these are important motives in the large corporation. "Satisficing" rather than maximizing criteria are usually applied, and the resulting slack or surplus in the system allows it to weather storms. This contributes to stability, if not to profits.[7] Indeed, the motivations and behavior of public and private bureaucrats appear to be more and more the same.

The attempt to differentiate public from private bureaucracies may be prompted by ideological considerations. The blanket insistence that public bureaucracy is inefficient may help to stem the advance of expanding government, and it

[4] Adolph A. Berle, Jr., and Gardiner C. Means: *The Modern Corporation and Private Property* (New York: The Macmillan Co.; 1932). For a discussion of the implications of the separation of ownership and control, see Wilbert E. Moore: *Industrial Relations and the Social Order*, rev. ed. (New York: The Macmillan Co.; 1951), pp. 56 ff.

[5] Berle and Means: op. cit. See also Robert A. Gordon: *Business Leadership in the Large Corporation* (Washington, D.C.: The Brookings Institution; 1945). Also George Thomas Washington and V. Henry Rothschild: *Compensating the Corporation Executive* (New York: The Ronald Press Company; 1951). These writers say that the data "appear to show the absence of any fixed relation between executive compensation and either profits or sales." The larger the profits, the smaller the share that goes to management. Conversely, the smaller the profits, the larger the share so paid out (ibid., p. 12). If the professional business manager's motivation is personal profit, it is obviously in conflict with the interests of stockholders.

[6] Gordon: op. cit.

[7] See March and Simon: op. cit., pp. 140-1. Maximizing requires a set of criteria which permits all alternatives to be compared. "Satisficing" requires only a set of minimal criteria, so that any one alternative may be selected or rejected without comparing it to all others.

may give some show of legitimacy to insecure business leaders who no longer enjoy the charismatic legitimations of their owner-operator predecessors.[8] The insistence that men are motivated to efficiency only by profit flies in the face of common sense and can no longer be used to differentiate and disparage the public bureaucrat. Finally, the disparagement of public bureaucracy may express the resentment of a recently alienated right wing in our society.

4. Bureaupathology

Associated with the general organizational characteristics of bureaucracy which arise from specialization, we find certain *personal-behavior* patterns which call for analysis. Everyone has met the pompous, self-important official at some time in his life, and many have served under autocratic, authoritarian superiors. Employees who seem to be interested in nothing but a minimal performance of their own little office routines are numerous enough, and impersonal treatment of clients and associates that approaches the coldness of absolute zero is not, sadly, uncommon. Such behavior patterns are personal rather than organizational: neither are they planned devices for achieving organizational goals nor do they achieve them. It is our contention that they reflect *personal* needs of insecure persons.

To the extent that such insecurity is a function of an individual's personality, it is of no concern to organization theory. To the extent, however, that it is a function of tensions normally generated in the bureaucratic organization, it must be accounted for in our theory. As we shall see in the following chapters, the growing imbalance between the rights of authority positions, on the one hand, and the abilities and skills needed in a technological age, on the other, generates tensions and insecurities in the system of authority. Attempts to reduce such insecurity often take the form of behavior patterns which are dysfunctional from the point of

[8] See Gouldner: op. cit., pp. 133 ff.

view of the organization, although functional enough from that of the insecure official. From the standpoint of the organization such behavior is pathological, and in our analysis we shall refer to it as *bureaupathic behavior.* As we shall see, the modern organization is a prolific generator of anxiety and insecurity. It would be difficult to imagine a more efficient one. Consequently, bureaupathic behavior is not exclusively associated with insecure personality types. It is found also in the "normal" personality of our assumed average organizational participant. Bureaupathic behavior, therefore, is a problem for organization theory rather than psychiatry. It is discussed at length in a later chapter.

In that later chapter we also discuss another phenomenon associated with bureaucracy. There are many people in our society who have not been able to adapt to bureaucracy and who, therefore, find it a constant and complete frustration. Theirs is a kind of social disease which we might call *bureausis.* "Bureautics" find the rationalism, orderliness, impartiality, and impersonality of the bureaucratic organization intolerable. They crave an immediate and tender response to their unique problems, whatever they may be. Bureautics are immature. They have never been weaned from habits of childhood indulgence. Bureautic behavior is not an organizational phenomenon. It is a function of the individual personality. Because it is associated with organizations, however, and is a reaction to them, and because it is the source of much misunderstanding of organizations, we believe we are justified in presenting a brief analysis of it.

To understand more fully the bureaucratic organization and the behavior we find within it, we turn our attention in the next chapter to the phenomenon of specialization; and after that to the hierarchy of authority, and to the relationship between specialization and hierarchy. It is in the struggle between these two elements that we find the reasons for much that interests us in our analysis. Whereas we were becoming conscious a generation or two ago of the divorcement of ownership from control, we are now becoming aware of a divorcement of management from control, as the result of advancing specialization.

CHAPTER 3

Specialization

♈

1. Specialization: Of Jobs and Men

A VAST AMOUNT of confusion can be avoided in our discussion of specialization if we distinguish at the outset between the specialization of tasks and the specialization of people. The first refers to the element of work specificity—making activities more specific—while the second refers to the adaptation of the individual to the conditions of his existence—increasing his chances for health and survival. In biology the term is used in this latter way, and this is the sense in which Emile Durkheim used it.[1] The specialized per-

[1] According to Durkheim the growth of density forced men to specialize in order to survive and also facilitated specialization by progressively narrowing the "common conscience" (similarities of psychological content). A new solidarity based upon the recognized mutual interdependence of specialists began to replace the old solidarity based on the common conscience. For this new kind of regulation of society to appear, "artificial" external obstacles to free specialization, such as caste, had to disappear. Otherwise the society would disintegrate because of lack of regulation, or normlessness, or "anomie." Each individual must be allowed to develop according to his capacities and aptitudes

son is adapted or changed. He can do things he could not do before and things that other people cannot do. If these things are valued by other people, his partial monopoly of ability to perform them gives him power. Other people are to some extent dependent upon him and must to that extent accommodate themselves to his needs. By virtue of his own behavior he can somewhat alter the satisfactions he receives from others.[2] His fate is not entirely beyond his own control.

Specialization of tasks, on the other hand, moves in the direction of the ever more specific, the narrowing of activities to simple, repetitive routines. It moves in the direction of the microdivision of labor, as for example, tightening bolts in an assembly line.

Performing such simple routines produces little change in the individual. Anyone can perform them, sometimes with a little practice but often without any at all if the job can be narrowed down sufficiently. The individual who performs such tasks acquires no power, of survival or otherwise. Nothing happens to him to increase the dependence of other people upon him. In short, he as a person does not become specialized by virtue of performing such specialized tasks.

If the prevailing technology does not allow an organization to specialize its tasks to the degree indicated above, performance of less specialized work will result in differentiation or specialization of the person himself who performs it. He will be changed; he will acquire skills and abilities

---

without the coercive restraints and distinctions of various differentiating social institutions. For society to achieve the new "organic" solidarity, there must be true equality of opportunity; there must be social justice. To Durkheim, specialization was nothing to be decried. It was a great, positive, moral force. *The Division of Labor in Society*, trans. George Simpson (New York: The Macmillan Co.; 1933). I have used the edition by The Free Press of Glencoe, Illinois, 1952; see ch. vi. Durkheim regarded modern solidarity as "organic" because it is based upon functional interdependence like the parts of an organism. Conversely, primitive solidarity was "mechanical."

[2] For a complete discussion of this point in technical terms of social psychology, see John W. Thibaut and Harold H. Kelley: *The Social Psychology of Groups* (New York: John Wiley & Sons, Inc.; 1959), ch. vii.

that other people do not have and would need some time to acquire. If such changes in the individual can be brought about in a relatively short time, the organization itself may undertake to bring them about, that is, to specialize the individual. In such case, the organization retains control of the kind of work he will perform.

If the existing technology requires a sufficiently more complex task to meet the organization's needs that the training period becomes impracticably longer, the organization must depend upon individuals who have been changed or specialized by activities and processes beyond its control, making the organization dependent upon other activities going on in the society. If an organization had all the resources necessary to differentiate or to specialize its own personnel, it would not be technically dependent upon any outside activities or upon the development of science and technology as a whole. The only "organization" which could achieve such a position of self-containment today is society itself. In fact, the development of science and technology is having in this respect a restrictive effect upon organizations. Bureaucratic organizations are increasingly losing control of their own job definitions to the social process of specialization. In general, we would say that the specialization of tasks is an organizational phenomenon ("the division of work"), while the specialization of people is a social process. Furthermore, task specialization and personal specialization are mutually antithetical. The more task specialization, the less personal specialization.

As we indicated above, the willingness to sacrifice personal specialization in the interests of task specialization depends ultimately upon the advance of science and technology. In the long run, man is man's greatest resource. In the short run, however, power may be used to thwart the full development of man. Anything that enables an organization to escape competition for survival may prolong technically backward task specialization and thus retard the full development of man's capacities. Under some circumstances of power (e.g., feudalism), technical development can itself be held back. Some revolutions in the historical past can be looked upon as moments of violence when privileged power positions were blasted away that were being used to prolong underutilization of people in relation to the current level of technological development, or even to retard technological progress itself. In a purely hypothetical state of evenly distributed power, survival of any enterprise would depend upon employment of the most highly developed individuals that the state of technological development would allow. The level of the individual's survival would depend upon the level of his development, that is, upon the degree of his adaptation or specialization. The level of survival of the society as a whole would be a result of the development of all its members to the highest level that the state of technological development would allow.[3]

2. *Specialization as a Social Process*

As we have said, the specialization of people is a social process, while task specialization is an organizational process. Jobs in an organization may be defined with due recognition to the social process. More and more are. However, there is also a great deal of planning of specialized tasks in organiza-

[3] Economic treatments of specialization from Adam Smith to the present time have emphasized task specialization and asserted that efficiency is increased by reducing the programs in the task. See, for example, Paul A. Samuelson: *Economics. An Introductory Analysis*, 1st ed. (New York: McGraw-Hill Book Co.; 1948), pp. 51-3. This result is explained as a consequence of reducing investment cost per unit of program execution. See James G. March and Herbert A. Simon: *Organizations* (New York: John Wiley & Sons, Inc.; 1958), p. 158. It is not our purpose to engage in polemics against this venerable tradition. However, its proponents should explain why, if this assertion is correct, task specialization and its corollary, the unskilled worker, disappear as science and technology advance. Are we becoming less efficient?

A few writers have recognized that task specialization is not the whole story. See, for example, Wilbert E. Moore and Arnold S. Feldman: *Labor Commitment and Social Change in Developing Areas* (New York: Social Science Research Council; 1960), pp. 29-31.

tions. This planning depends upon the superior power of the organization; such jobs are imposed.

The social process, the specialization of persons, goes on under the guiding influence of certain personal and social needs. Durkheim said that the individual specializes in order to survive satisfactorily within altered conditions of existence. In the absence of artificial restraints, he finds an activity compatible with his constitution, with his capacities and his tastes, which allows him to survive. One of the conditioning forces, therefore, is individual welfare. But specialization also contributes to social cohesion by impelling men to a recognition of their mutual interdependence. In purely organizational terms, we would say that these two sets of needs, personal and social, simply reflect the fact that organizational arrangements must meet at least minimally the personal goals of the participants and the formal, objective, external goal of the organization. Although there are obvious theoretical difficulties in such a formulation, it helps to think of the organization as a means to the participants' goals and the participants as means to the organization's goals. Cohesion is an organizational need because the interdependence created by specialization makes the accomplishment of the organization's goal dependent upon co-operation at the same time that it destroys the older interpersonal bonds of the common conscience. The dependence of the organization's goal upon co-operation grows more intense as specialization progresses.

Specialization meets the needs of the individual when it contributes to his survival, by which we mean the survival of the values and aspirations which constitute him as a human being—a good deal more than the mere perpetuation of life. Special abilities may remove a person from some competition, thereby increasing his power and his control over his own destiny. In order for such differentiation to increase the individual's power, he must be able to do socially valued things that not everyone can do. He must acquire a social *function*. However, an individual's values would not survive well unless his function were compatible with both his capacities *and* his tastes, unless the function were to some extent an end as well as a means. If, as Thibaut and Kelley argue, a person's prestige is a result of the relative amount of satisfactions believed to result from his activities, we can assume that a function consistent with a person's attitudes and tastes will provide him greater prestige or status than will distasteful activities.[4] The needs of the individual, therefore, guide specialization along lines of increased status and function for the individual.[5] Increased status and function, in turn, imply an individual who is modified or developed to the limits of his capacities and attitudes; in short, a specialized individual.

We assume that if conditions permitted, most people would seek to enlarge their status and function, which implies considerable self-development differentiating them from others. The empirically observed bases for job satisfactions lend verification to this assumption. As March and Simon summarize these observations,[6] job satisfaction is greater when the following conditions prevail:

[4] Op. cit., ch. xii. The individual must find a conflict-free capacity which, because it is independent of his personality, he can guide cognitively in the pursuit of various ends other than his own. He must, in other words, find a capacity which he can use well, without pain and, in fact, with the enjoyment of healthy, effective effort. With such a capacity he can "survive" and "succeed." It will help him to achieve an identity; it will provide him with status and function. See Erik Homburger Erikson: "The Problem of Ego Identity," *J. Am. Psychoanalytic Assoc.*, Vol. IV (1956), pp. 58-121, reproduced in Maurice R. Stein, Arthur J. Vidich, and David Manning White, eds.: *Identity and Anxiety* (Glencoe, Illinois: The Free Press; 1960), pp. 37-87.

[5] "The realization of human dignity, the achievement of status and function would thus emerge as the major unanswered question of industrial society." Peter Drucker: *Concept of the Corporation* (New York: The John Day Co.; 1946), p. 152. Harold Laswell makes such a wide sharing of status and function the basis of his definition of a democratic society. See *Power and Personality* (New York: W. W. Norton & Company, Inc.; 1948), p. 9.

[6] Op. cit., pp. 76-7, 94-7. The importance of many of these listed items lies in the fact that they relate to "finding oneself," to acquiring an identity. This, we believe, is the personal significance of a career. See Erikson: loc. cit.

1. The job requires a high level of skill.
2. The job requires the use of a number of different programs rather than one or a few.
3. The work role is compatible with the employee's self-image and his nonwork roles.
4. The job is considered to be a career.
5. There is considerable autonomy in decision.
6. Work relations are predictable.
7. The organization has less control over the job (that is to say, the job is less organizationally defined).

In other words, an occupation provides more satisfaction to the individual when it provides him with status and function and with some power or control over his destiny.

Specialization meets relevant social needs to the extent that it preserves or promotes the amount of co-operation needed to achieve organizational goals under conditions of increasing interdependence which, in turn, result from advancing specialization. The nature of these guiding social needs can be determined by discovering the conditions which make interdependence more or less tolerable. Experimental studies with small groups show that the toleration of specialization, hence interdependence, is increased as the cohesion of the group increases.[7] Some of these studies also show that group cohesion is increased when relationships within the group are governed by democratic rather than autocratic norms and when each person is interested in the group's activities as a whole.[8] The microdivision of work, or

[7] For example, see M. Deutsch: "An Experimental Study of the Effects of Cooperation and Competition upon Group Processes," *Human Relations*, Vol. II (1949), pp. 199-232; K. Back: "The Exertion of Influence Through Social Communication," *J. Abnormal Psychol.*, Vol. XLVI (1951), pp. 9-23; S. Schachter: "Deviation, Rejection and Communication," *J. Abnormal Psychol.*, Vol. XLVI (1951), pp. 190-207.

[8] In addition to the references in the preceding footnote, see R. Lippitt: "An Experimental Study of Authoritarian and Democratic Group Atmospheres," in *University of Iowa Studies in Child Welfare*, Vol. XVI, No. 3 (1940); also Kurt Lewin: *Resolving Social Conflicts* (New York: Harper & Brothers; 1948). Studies of the differential impact of democratic and autocratic norms and practices upon group functioning have not produced entirely consistent results.

task specialization, makes it difficult to see the relationship between individual activity and group activity.[9] Jobs which do not meet the needs of the individual and which must be autocratically imposed are not likely by themselves to contribute to social cohesion.[1]

The solidarity of the small group is a solidarity of affect or, as Durkheim would say, one based upon likeness rather than differentiation. In the broader community of specialists, while the remaining common elements or likenesses will play their part, a more rational basis for the integration of the community must be found. This basis, according to Durkheim, is the recognized mutual interdependence of specialists.

It is not enough for the interdependence to be perceived; it must be recognized as necessary or else it would not be tolerated under conditions of free choice. The interdependence, therefore, must be based upon tacit agreement, at least. An interdependence which was perceived as unnecessary, as escapable, would have to be arbitrarily imposed and maintained by superior power, because the power of the individual would be increased by escaping it. We pointed out above that individual needs influence specialization by motivating people to find important social functions which other people cannot perform for themselves. The resulting interdependence is real, not spurious (i.e., it is intellectually inescapable); it is acceptable because it is seen to be necessary. It would appear, therefore, that the effects of individual needs and social needs upon the social process of specialization are reinforcing. Both sets of guiding influences work in the direction of greater individual development, greater individual differentiation, greater individual power of survival, and greater individual status and function. Specialization creates difficulties associated with interdependence which can

---

[9] See Wilbert E. Moore: *Industrial Relations and the Social Order*, rev. ed. (New York: The Macmillan Co.; 1951), pp. 228 ff.; Georges Friedman: *Industrial Society* (Glencoe, Illinois: The Free Press; 1955).

[1] However, a working group whose activities have been divided in such a way may find nonjob group interests and activities which are likely to conflict with formal organization norms. See Moore: op. cit., pp. 264-70; Friedman: op. cit.; March and Simon: op. cit.

be summed up as the problem of co-operation. Task specialization, or the microdivision of labor, aggravates this problem. Personal specialization holds the hope of its solution. It is reassuring to note that the historical offspring of task specialization, the unskilled laborer, is rapidly being eliminated from the scene.

The distinction between task specialization and personal specialization helps to clear up some ambiguities in the concept of specialization. As to whether the assembly-line worker who turns nut no. 48 all day long is more or less specialized than the plant engineer, we can easily see that the former is not a specialized person at all, while the latter assuredly is. The assembly-line worker is not a changed or modified person by virtue of his job. Anyone could perform it. He gets no survival power from his function; he has not reduced his competition. He has little status and function. On the other hand, the engineer is a developed and differentiated individual with much greater power of survival, much reduced competition, and a greater function and status. The *task* of the assembly-line worker, however, is much more specialized than that of the engineer.

3. The Program and Job Analysis

The analysis of specialization is further aided by the concept of a "program." As the "therblig" was an attempt to define a unit of physical action (e.g., lifting, putting down, etc.), so the "program" is meant to be a unit of purposive action. It is an organized and fairly complex set of activities of a goal-achieving kind. When internalized in the individual, programs are called skills. When committed to paper, they are procedures. Among other things, a profession is a number of interrelated programs, the use of which is governed by an occupational ethic. Programs vary according to their complexity, according to whether they are more manual or more intellectual, and according to the social value attached to them. Functions (tasks, jobs, occupations) vary according to the number of programs involved, their complexity, their intellectuality, and their social evaluation. Consequently, functions also vary according to the time needed to acquire them. People vary biologically and sociopsychologically in their ability to master a given function in a given period of time. A completely specialized task would contain a single program. The function of a specialized person contains a great many programs, the number limited by their complexity and by the capacity of the individual. Consequently, as bodies of knowledge (intellectual programs) or techniques expand beyond the capacities of most of the people who are specialized in them, new functions or specialties appear which seem to be subdivisions of the older ones. These new specialties do not constitute task specialization—the reduction of the number of programs in a task. They have either more programs or more complicated programs than the older specialty, or both. These new specialties consistently take a longer time to master than the older ones out of which they have grown. It takes longer to become a "specialist" than a "general practitioner." The period of preparation for one's social function is growing longer; the school-leaving age is advancing. These changes reflect the advance of personal specialization and the decline of task specialization. Nevertheless, specializing the task makes it possible to find some indispensable function which fits the capacities of the most limited individual. Everyone can acquire some power if permitted to do so. Everyone can be to some extent specialized.

The fact that the number and complexity of programs a person can master is limited helps to explain the relationship between specialization and bureaucracy. As business knowledge and techniques accumulated, the early merchant-producer or owner-manager found he could not perform his function well enough to meet competition, even operating at the peak of his capacity. New business functions or specialties which seem to be subdivisions of the original owner-manager function have appeared. These new business functions do not represent a parceling out of the programs performed by the former manager. They contain new programs from the growing body of knowledge and techniques.

The specialists who have mastered these new specialties are not lesser men who perform fewer and simpler programs than the former managers. Their preparation for their functions takes longer. Experts in purchasing, transportation, finance, law, engineering, personnel, and many others have appeared. More and more the intellectual or decision-making functions of the organization are shifted to these new specialists, reducing the manager's function more and more to the pure exercise of authority. As these new functions continue to develop and more specialists appear, it becomes necessary to group or departmentalize them. The organization grows in size and acquires a complex structure of "bureaus" of specialized people. A greater and greater proportion of the organization's total personnel consists of people performing these new functions or specialties, with a smaller and smaller proportion of people performing physical production programs. The same processes and forces determine the evolution of governmental organizations. From these various changes the bureaucratic form of organization emerges.[2]

4. Job Planning

To a considerable extent modern bureaucracy is composed of specialties and specialists as the *social process* of specialization has provided them. It reflects the social structure of the trades and professions. However, a certain amount of *conscious planning* of jobs takes place within organizations. The conscious planning of tasks involves the combination of programs into jobs. Unless programs become grouped to-

[2] The following figures illustrate the tempo of these changes. Between 1947 and 1958 the number of production workers in manufacturing industries in this country went down 9 per cent, while the number of nonproduction workers went up 50 per cent. Unskilled workers were 36 per cent of the labor force in 1910, but only 19.9 per cent in 1957. United States Congress, Joint Economic Committee: *Staff Report on Employment, Growth, and Price Levels*, 86th Cong., 1st Sess. (1959).

gether into jobs by chance or accident, there are always in the various programs elements which are in some way complementary to one another and which suggest or promote the grouping into a specific job. The number of ways programs may be combined together is limited only by human ability to perceive a number of elements as a unity. Programs may be combined together in one job because "they always have been" (traditional grouping); because some of the same words are used in the titles of the programs (semantic grouping); because both can be included in the same class of programs (conceptual grouping); because they complement one another esthetically (esthetic grouping); because each can achieve its planned goal better in association with the other (instrumental grouping); and for many other reasons. If three machines, A, B, and C, each produced all three products, 1, 2, and 3, a certain amount of time would be lost on each machine changing over from 1 to 2, from 2 to 3, and from 3 to 1 again. If all programs concerning product 1 were assigned to machine A, product 2 to machine B, and product 3 to machine C, this loss of "change-over" time could be avoided. Such a grouping would be an *instrumental* one.

The accomplishment of objective, externalized goals is associated with a continuous effort to combine programs on an instrumental basis. It has become customary to refer to this continuous effort as "rationalization." Although we are primarily concerned with the division of work on the basis of instrumental considerations, the reader should never forget that a great deal of organizational planning is based upon semantic and conceptual considerations. It is hard to miss the semantic overtones in the First Hoover Commission's recommendation to transfer the Bureau of Commercial Fisheries from the Department of the Interior to the Department of Commerce. And the major components of the Department of Health, Education and Welfare bear a relationship to one another which is chiefly conceptual in nature.

Although the measurement of accomplishment necessarily stresses objective, externalized goals and therefore combinations based on instrumental considerations, it is important to remember that the *personal* satisfactions of participants are just as likely to be associated with other kinds of combinations. It has been reported to us that it took one of the great press associations about a year to switch its reporters from yellow to green copy paper in order to minimize glare in the eyes of employees. The latter, for reasons of their own, preferred yellow paper. It has never been possible to rationalize the spelling of the English language. We are told that when President Theodore Roosevelt tried to introduce simplified spellings, the United States Supreme Court announced that it would refuse to consider cases so recorded. There are limits to the extent to which a kitchen can be rationalized, because the housewife has certain preferences based upon traditional, esthetic, and sentimental considerations. The advance of bureaucracy and rationalization has tended to blind us to the fact that personal satisfactions are less a function of goals than of process. As a result of this blindness on our part, programs are for the most part combined into jobs on the basis of instrumental considerations alone, thereby destroying "joy in work" for millions and millions of persons.

Although instrumental considerations are stressed in the conscious planning of jobs, this planning is subject to a number of limiting factors. In schematic terms, problems subject to conscious task planning are factored or analyzed into a means-end map. The problem is first reduced to the general means for its solution. Each of these means, in turn, treated as a subgoal, is further reduced to *its* means, and so on until concrete programs are reached.[3] These programs must then be grouped into tasks or jobs. The limiting considerations mentioned above apply to this last step; and they are economic, biopsychological, cultural, and social in nature. A job with too many different programs assigned to it involves costs in switching from one program to another. A job with too few involves the costs of dead time because there is not sufficient demand for the programs.[4] A job with too many

[3] See March and Simon: op. cit., *passim.*
[4] See Herbert A. Simon, Donald W. Smithburg, and Victor A. Thompson: *Public Administration* (New York: Alfred A. Knopf;

programs will be beyond an individual's capacity to master. A job with too few will result in boredom.[5] Another limitation on task planning arises from definitions associated with hierarchy. The hierarchical relationship is a monocratic one. The superior is to be the *only* person in the organization who has the right to deal with the subordinate, especially the right to communicate with the subordinate and to tell him what to do. Programs must be allocated to jobs in such a way that the jobs will fit into this monocratic framework. The individual must find himself in the subordinate relationship to only one superior. His job cannot combine programs to be performed in unit A with programs to be performed in unit B without violating the monocratic expectations of the hierarchical institution. The reader will recognize the relationship between these monocratic expectations and the expression "unity of command." Jobs must be defined in such a way that they can be "completely" fitted into *supervisory units*. We have put quotes around "completely" because no job can actually be so defined. The programs in the job will always have complementary relationships and, especially, instrumental relationships with programs in other jobs beyond the supervisory unit. It may be true that the institutional framework of our society *encourages* instrumental groupings, but the only kind it *commands* is the authoritative grouping. Semantic, esthetic, ideological, traditional, and other groupings in addition to the instrumental are both possible and quite common.

In addition to the various limitations discussed above, there are also severe social constraints on the conscious planning of tasks or jobs. A new specialty—a job with relatively new and untried programs—is viewed with suspicion and even hostility by established specialists. The new may threaten the old with loss of functions or programs, and therefore with the loss of status. Individuals are usually not able to evaluate new specialties, and they depend upon

---

1950), ch. vi. See also Adam Smith, *The Wealth of Nations*, who pointed out that specialization was limited by the size of markets.

[5] Simon, Smithburg, and Thompson: op. cit.

various social-accreditation mechanisms to do this for them. These mechanisms develop slowly, and it takes time for a new specialty to "win its spurs." An established specialist enjoys a socially accepted function and status which might be endangered by the acceptance of new functions. He therefore resists attempts to unload new programs upon him; whereas the new specialist, with neither socially accepted function nor status, is often eager for new programs, since he has everything to win and nothing to lose.[6]

Both new and old specialists will, however, resist additional programs which have a low social evaluation, because of possible adverse effects upon status, and because performing such programs is not likely to be enjoyable. For example, it would be safe to predict that the bureau economist would resist the assignment of janitorial programs to his job. Both new and old specialists will also resist loss of functions, because of adverse effects upon status, and because loss of functions means loss of survival power—it means that the individual is less specialized, and that society is therefore less dependent upon him.[7]

5. *Centralization*

When new specialties become available, some old ones must lose functions, even becoming obsolete in the extreme case. In this sense, specialization is the same as centralization: many become dependent for these functions on the few new specialists. For example, suppose we have a mine with no formally recognized safety department. Each worker decides for himself how best to maintain safety on the job. Then a new safety technology appears and with it a new specialist, the safety engineer. When the mine superintendent hires a safety engineer, the workers lose the associated

[6] See below ch. v.

[7] Among the services of a professional association is the protection of the function and status of its members, even to the extent of defining precisely how its members may be used in organizations. Craft unions provide the same service to their members.

function. We would say that the safety function has been *centralized* to the mine level. The many have become dependent upon the one new specialist.

Within organizations, new specialties can be economically utilized only if sufficient demand can be concentrated to employ fully the new specialists. Activities may therefore be centralized because of the continuing advance of specialization. However, activities are also frequently centralized for other reasons; for example, for esthetic reasons, or as a reward to the winners of a power struggle.

A technology at a particular stage of development requires a particular degree of centralization in order to fulfill its promise. We can think of this degree of centralization as a function of the stage of development of the technology, or, what is the same for practical purposes, the existing state of specialization in the society. If centralization is carried beyond this instrumentally required level, needs other than those arising from the technology are clearly at work. Such needs arise or press for recognition at the point of authority where the right to carry centralization to this level is located. To understand such centralization one must understand the needs in question. Often such needs relate to the desire for personal power and status; sometimes they may be traced to a demand for uniformity or for the recognition of particularistic interests or values. As we shall argue in a later chapter, they are perhaps most frequently related to personal insecurity, particularly insecurity generated by the structure of the bureaucratic organization. Such centralization is carried out by political rather than analytical processes and relates to personal goals or values rather than to the formal, objective goals of the organization. Since it is not generally acceptable throughout the organization, it must be imposed by authority. In short, centralization may be the natural result of specialization, or it may be an arbitrary creation by someone with superior power.

To illustrate these propositions, let us assume that three divisions within a department all have a demand for the services of an electronic computer, but that none of them has sufficient demand to employ a computer for more than a few hours a day. The department could not afford three partly employed computers and so would have to do without their specialized services unless it centralized them into a new computer division. It makes good sense to regard the centralization of computer services under such circumstances as a function of advancing technology. On the other hand, if each division had sufficient demand fully to employ a computer, centralizing these services into a new computer division would not be a result of the process of specialization but a result rather of needs of a different nature surrounding the position of the head of the department. It is not necessary to specify these needs. The important point is that in the first illustration the centralization was intellectually inescapable, while in the second it was at least arguable. In the first it was acceptable, while in the second it may not have been and most likely was not. In the first illustration the centralization was a by-product of technical and scientific progress, while in the second it was imposed by power or authority.

From a technological point of view, failure to use needed and available products of specialization in men or machines is "overdecentralization," as when a man tries to be his own doctor. On the other hand, centralization beyond what is technologically indicated, as in one of the computer examples above, is "overcentralization." It is suspected by many people that overcentralization is rampant in the industrial part of the world, that power needs of particular individuals are probably as prominent as technical needs of working units in determining many of our organizational arrangements.

6. *Departmentalization*

When we discussed job planning above, we pointed out that the number of ways programs can be combined together into jobs is limited only by the ability to perceive a number of elements as a unity. The same considerations apply to departmentalization—the broader grouping of jobs into units, units into larger units, larger units into still larger units, etc.

Departmentalization is also a perceptual problem, and the number of ways to departmentalize is likewise limited only by the ability to perceive a number of elements as a unity. Thus, particular departmental groupings are frequently associated with the assertion that "like activities should be in the same place." Since the organizational structure tells us about authority relations but *not* about geographic ones, "the same place" refers to *the same place on an organization chart*. In other words, the titles of the activities in question should all appear in one box on the chart. The only organizational significance of this grouping is to determine the point at which conflicts concerning these "like activities" will be finally resolved. Of course, if the activities in question have instrumental relationships with one another, the organizational location of the point of final settlement of conflicts concerning them may itself be an instrumental problem, because the need for such final conflict settlement may be great. The settlement of such conflicts may intimately affect the accomplishment of the organizational goal. However, common experience suggests that many of the conflicts requiring final settlement in our bureaucratic organizations relate to personal goals rather than to organizational ones. Angry men battle with words over organizationally irrelevant issues cloaked in the rhetoric of organizational necessity. When such issues are debated as whether school health activities, for example, should be "placed in" the department of health or the department of education, it is quite possible that the needs at stake are perceptual or otherwise, and not at all related to the accomplishment of organizational goals.[8] Arguments about departmentalization are frequently stimu-

[8] If the school system has a large enough demand for health services to employ fully the latest relevant specializations in people and equipment, it makes no technical difference in which department school health activities are located. The decision will be made on grounds of tradition, semantics, or what not. It will be made by political, power processes rather than rational, analytic processes. Those favoring the transfer will attempt to show that economies will be realized. Those opposing will attempt to show that costs will go up. Both arguments will be spurious.

lated by traditional, semantic, esthetic, or other considerations, under conditions which have no instrumental implications whatsoever.

The kind of departmentalization existing in an organization results either from the process of specialization or from acts of power. Further light is thrown upon this subject by considering the causes of interdependence. The literature on departmentalization suggests that interdependence is created by the organization planner rather than by specialization. It is said to be a result of departmentalizing by process rather than by purpose. In this literature the distinction between a purpose and a process is never made clear, but we assume that a purpose is an end product, a socially valued result, and that a process is one of the means for achieving this result. Today, people specialize by process almost entirely, so that any particular function or job is almost certain to be a process, that is, a means to some socially valued end product. The advance of specialization differentiates people on the basis of process. In an earlier period, there were product specialists —craftsmen like shoemakers, hatters, etc. As the programs within these various product specialties increased beyond the capacities of individual specialists, new process specialists began to appear. (Other forces aided in the elimination of such crafts, as we point out in the last part of this chapter.) Today there are relatively few product specialists left in advanced industrial societies. Perhaps some jewelers may be considered product specialists. Some product specialties have survived only by meeting new social needs for education or entertainment. Glass-blowing might be an example. Even here, however, it is probably more accurate to regard this activity as a process specialty, since the end product is scientific research or even entertainment rather than glass containers for home use.[9]

[9] "The very rapid evolution during the past 30 years of the glass and mirror industry, the present very technical aspect of manufacture and means of scientific control, have transformed the trade of the glassmaker, who has nothing in common with his former self. The men at Chantereine today are controllers, estimators, electronic experts, mechanics, oven supervisors, operators of tractors or traveling cranes

As the production of the end product comes to require the combined activities of several process specialists, interdependence and the need for co-ordination arises. Interdependence is therefore a result of advancing specialization. Regardless of how the process specialists are grouped into organizational units, regardless of how they are departmentalized, the amount of technical interdependence between the relevant programs and between the specialists who embody them will be the same. It is not in any way affected by the methods of departmentalization. However, the level or location of the formal authority to settle conflicts arising out of this interdependence will vary according to the method of departmentalization used. Furthermore, any one method used will send a particular question higher for settlement than would another method, and another question lower. When the jobs are not themselves changed, the reallocation of jobs to units, in addition to changing the level of conflict settlement, has only the *formal* consequence of changing the person who is the boss of the persons performing the jobs. It will certainly also have indeterminate *informal* consequences, since it will affect the interpersonal communication patterns somewhat and will in any case be subject to critical evaluation on the part of the human beings involved in the reallocation.

To illustrate these points, let us suppose an organization, X, has two departments, A and B, each of which has jobs or activities, 1 and 2. A has jobs A_1 and A_2; B has jobs B_1 and B_2. The organization, X, is then reorganized so that it has two departments, 1 and 2, each of which has jobs A and B. Department 1 has A_1 and B_1; department 2 has A_2 and B_2. The interdependence between the activities A_1, A_2, B_1, and B_2 has not been affected by the reorganization. It is determined by the technology underlying the jobs. The levels,

---

... yet the glassmaker's trade has preserved its particular spirit, built upon devotion to the trade and to the sense of teamwork, and has kept its traditions." Robert Caussin: "The Transfer of Functions from Man to Machine," *Diogenes* (winter, 1959), pp. 117-18, quoted in United States Congress, Joint Economic Committee: *New Views on Automation*, 86th Cong., 2nd Sess. (1960), p. 63.

however, at which particular kinds of conflicts are authoritatively resolved have been changed by the reorganization. Under the original departmentalization, conflicts A_1-A_2 and B_1-B_2 were resolvable at the departmental level, while conflicts A_1-B_1 and A_2-B_2 were resolvable at the very top. After reorganization, conflict A_1-A_2 and B_1-B_2 could be finally settled only at the very top, while A_1-B_1 and A_2-B_2 could be settled at the departmental level.

If all the process specialties needed to produce a given socially valued end product could be placed in one unit, that unit, by definition, would be departmentalized by purpose rather than by process. If more than one unit is needed to produce this end product, each of these units, again by definition, is departmentalized by process, while the larger unit which contains them both is a purpose organization. At some level, every organization represents departmentalization by purpose, since we define the organization in terms of an end product, a socially valued goal. All of the components below this level represent departmentalization by process.

Whether any particular level is the purpose level depends either upon specialization or upon the power system within the organization. Below some level, all of the relevant specialties in people and equipment can be fully employed. This is the level which the existing state of science and technology decrees shall be the level of purpose departmentalization. However, for various reasons, as we have seen above, centralization may be carried beyond this point by authority, creating technically unnecessary interdependence. It is also true that tasks or jobs which create technically unnecessary interdependence may be imposed by authority. In both these cases, the purpose level will be higher than is technically necessary. Furthermore, those in authority may decide to forego the advantages of specialization in the hope of avoiding the co-ordination costs of interdependence. They may not centralize to the extent which the prevailing technologies require. In the absence of contrary evidence, however, we suspect that the advantages of specialization always outweigh the associated costs of co-ordination. Although a given organization may be too small at any one time to avail itself of the existing level of specialization in society, we suspect that this condition is temporary. The organization will expand, merge with others, or disappear. We conclude again that the amount of interdependence and the kind of departmentalization existing in any particular organization result either from the social process of specialization or from acts of power.

7. *Specialization and the Status System*

We pointed out above that personal specialization makes it possible to find a necessary function for everyone, the old and the young, those with great and those with limited capacities. It is therefore inevitable that essential programs will be performed by persons of low as well as high status. As a consequence, interdependence between persons of higher and lower status is inevitable, and this violates the understandings and expectations which underlie the status system. (These expectations are discussed in the next chapter.) Whereas task specialization, the microdivision of work, also creates interdependence, it is not so violative of the status system as interstratum interdependence which results from personal specialization. The dependence of the higher-status person in the case of task specialization is a dependence upon an abstract task rather than upon a person, because the person who performs the task can be easily replaced. Furthermore, the dependence is hidden by procedures and does not involve much face-to-face accommodation. More and more, however, organizational interdependence involves personal specialization and with it the dependence of higher-status persons upon lower-status persons. In these conditions, the high-status persons must accord face-to-face accommodation to lower-status persons. This accommodation violates status expectations.[1]

[1] This point is illustrated by the relations between physicians and the paramedical professionals in hospitals. These subprofessionals—for example, laboratory technicians—"will talk back to the doctors and not let them browbeat them." Albert F. Wessen: "Hospital Ideology and

Alongside the relationship of technical *interdependence* in modern organizations is the older relationship of *dependence*, the man-boss relationship. This relationship will be explored in the next chapter. Here we wish only to point out that this relationship is formally unilateral. It is formally a relationship of dependence rather than of interdependence and is therefore demeaning for the subordinate, at least in our culture. The relationship of technical interdependence, on the other hand, is essentially an exchange relationship. Each side has something to offer the other; each, therefore, has power over the other. Each side prospers from the exchange, so that the relationship is positive, facilitative, rewarding. Whereas the boss-man relationship is *formally* unilateral with rights running in one direction from the boss to the man, the advance of personal specialization is converting the relationship *informally* into a unilateral one with ability running from the man to the boss. Authority is centralized, but ability is inherently decentralized because it comes from practice rather than from definition. Whereas the boss retains his full *rights* to make all decisions, he has less and less *ability* to do so because of the advance of science and technology. For these reasons the man-boss relationship has become curiously distorted and unstable; formally unilateral boss-to-man, informally unilateral man-to-boss. Each has power in the relationship, but the power of the man does not have the sanction of legitimacy.[2]

Communication between Ward Personnel," in E. Gartly Jaco, ed.: *Patients, Physicians and Illness* (Glencoe, Illinois: The Free Press; 1958), p. 455.

[2] On the lack of congruence between the structure of technical ability ("power") and the structure of authority, see James D. Thompson: "Authority and Power in 'Identical' Organizations," *Am. J. Sociol.* (November 1956), reprinted in *Comparative Studies in Administration*, edited by the Staff of the Administrative Science Center, University of Pittsburgh (University of Pittsburgh Press; 1959), p. 35. "Major deviations of power structures from authority structures apparently came about because of the *technical requirements* of operations rather than because of personal relations." (Italics ours.)

8. Co-ordination

Since specialization creates interdependence, it creates the need for co-ordination. In an earlier period, the person with most abilities concerning a particular activity, the person who had mastered all programs relevant to the activity, could be given the authority with regard to it. He could co-ordinate the behavior of others by command. They needed only to do what he told them to do. Although the monistic model still projects this primitive pattern, the accumulation of knowledge and techniques has far outrun the ability of individuals to co-ordinate in this fashion, except for some supervisors of highly specialized tasks. The microdivision of work preserves the primitive, monistic, autocratic practice of administration by command. For most administration, however, co-ordination must be achieved by programming interdependent activities, and this is achieved by procedures or routines. Jurisdictions are established; categories for classifying program-evoking information are defined; programs appropriate to each category are worked out; temporal and spatial sequences of activities are built into these programs; and feed-back communication procedures for handling deviations from planned or predicted activities or conditions are installed. We find, therefore, the "rules and regulations" so characteristic of modern bureaucracy. Like any other organizational device, these rules and regulations may be therapeutic or antitherapeutic. They may be consistent with the personal goals of participants, or they may block these goals. They may reduce tension because they meet an apparent operational need, because they result from the recognition of mutual interdependence. On the other hand, the rules and regulations may increase tensions if they constitute an imposed division of work emphasizing jurisdictions or rights rather than abilities. Here again we note the possibility of conflict between specialization and authority. The nature and causes of this conflict will be discussed in the next two chapters.

First, however, we shall illustrate some of the propositions we have stated in this chapter by discussing two examples: one of personal specialization, and the other of task specialization.

9. Personal Specialization

The social process of personal specialization is well illustrated by differentiation within the medical profession, a differentiation which has taken place almost entirely within the last century. The *American Medical Directory* for 1942 notes the following medical specialties: surgery, obstetrics, gynecology, neurological surgery, orthopedic surgery, plastic surgery, proctology, anesthesia, pediatrics, internal medicine, ophthalmology, otology, laryngology, rhinology, psychiatry, neurology, dermatology, urology, roentgenology, radiology, pathology, bacteriology, and anatomy.

Differentiation within medicine has resulted from the development of medical science and techniques. "When appropriate instruments were invented, medical science expanded to such an extent that specialists became a necessity, for no man could master the field of medicine in its entirety." [3] The differentiating process was not *planned* either by schools or by hospitals; they *responded* to it. The ophthalmoscope, invented in 1851, was brought to this country in 1855 by Dr. Elkanah Williams of Cincinnati, the first ophthalmologist in this country. Departments of ophthalmology in medical schools appeared later—Cincinnati in 1860, Bellevue in 1868, Rush in 1869, Northwestern in 1870, Harvard in 1871, and Pennsylvania in 1872. The nonorganizational origin of specialization is further underlined by the fact that the individual physician's decision to specialize arises, for the most part, out of experiences in medical practice. As the years go by, more and more of any particular

[3] Bernhard J. Stern: *American Medical Practice in the Perspectives of a Century* (New York: The Commonwealth Fund; 1945), p. 45.

graduating class of physicians will become specialists, showing that "the causes of increased specialization are to be
found more in the conditions of professional life in which
the medical graduate finds himself than in the orientation he
receives in medical school." [4] Specialization has been a response to personal needs of practicing physicians. "Larger
incomes and wider opportunities to advance the scientific
frontiers of medicine and to obtain public and professional
recognition have increased the number of specialists." [5]

In medicine, as elsewhere, new specialties are resisted
by established specialists because of fear of loss of function. The new specialist "risks . . . the resentment of the
other physicians who feel that their competence is being
challenged and their source of income curtailed." [6] Dr. Morton first used his painkillers in 1846, but the American Society of Anesthesiologists was not formally established until
1939. Beginning with the heroic efforts of Dr. Frank Mc-
Mechan in 1915, anesthesiologists have waged a strenuous
fight to win acceptance as a medical specialty, and their
battle is not over yet. Within the hospitals their potential
services were often overlooked, and in the distribution of
the budget they were slighted.

As medical practice has become more specialized, it has
become more impersonal, as we would expect.[7] It has also become more interdependent. This growing interdependence
and the fact that individual physicians cannot afford partly
employed and increasingly expensive medical equipment are
enhancing the importance of the hospital's role in medical
practice. Specialization requires organization. In the long run,
we expect medical practice to become largely bureaucratized.

[4] Milton Terries and Mary Monk: "Changes in Physicians' Careers: Relation of Time after Graduation to Specialization," *J. Am.
Med. Assoc.*, Vol. CLX (1956), p. 655.

[5] Stern: op. cit., p. 49.

[6] Stern: op. cit., p. 46. Many established physicians would not
associate socially with the first doctors of "the eye alone." Ibid.

[7] See Stern: op. cit.; and G. Canby Robinson: *The Patient as a
Person* (New York: The Commonwealth Fund; 1939).

The importance of group action to achieve and protect status and function is well illustrated by the anesthesiologists. Not very many years ago this function was generally assigned to nurses. The expansion of the technology by itself was not believed to be enough to win recognition for this new specialty, although it certainly would have been in time. The struggle for recognition took the form of a crusade. All devices of public relations and advertising were used, until the crusaders were finally restrained by fellow physicians for allegedly unethical conduct.

Eventually collective bargaining and even strikes were resorted to, although these practices were not reported in the press, or at least not in that terminology.[8] The crusaders found it more expedient to attack the hospital administration than their fellow physicians, and that became the focal point of their strategy. But what has undoubtedly helped them most is the steady onward advance of medical knowledge and techniques. The desire of a few physicians to specialize in anesthesiology could be overlooked as long as the technology was limited and its contribution small. But when anesthesiology became a matter of life and death, when it became a very important function, anesthesiologists acquired function and status. "The group which wants to differentiate itself in acceptable fashion can do so by constant elaboration of its technical arsenal. With each advance it becomes more useful to others and is thus accorded greater recognition."[9] Anesthesiologists, as would be expected of new specialists, have been eager for new functions and responsibilities in the hospitals, taking over most innovations designed to maintain the general condition of the patient in the operat-

8 See Dan C. Lortie: "Anesthesia: From Nurse's Work to Medical Specialty," in E. Gartly Jaco, ed.: *Patients, Physicians and Illness* (Glencoe, Illinois: The Free Press; 1958), pp. 405-12. The anesthesiologists managed to convince many of their fellow physicians that salary arrangements in hospitals were "group practice" and hence the beginning of "socialized medicine." Ibid.

9 Ibid., p. 412. "Gradually the task became redefined as one involving life and death." Ibid., p. 408.

ing room, and often following him outside by administering blood banks or "post-operative recovery rooms." [1] The elaboration of the anesthesiologist's functions have been in the direction of a more "doctor-like" posture and have served to widen the gap between the medical anesthetist and the nurse. They have been in the direction of increased function and status.

The history of differentiation in medicine shows that specialization is a social process. It cannot be understood on purely economic or rational grounds, but is a response to the complex needs of individuals as they face the experiences of life. As Durkheim said, we specialize in order to survive satisfactorily. This history shows that specialization and technological development are reciprocally related. Each depends upon and influences the other. It shows that specialization results in loss of authoritative control by established organizations as the specialists band together in organizations of their own. The new specialists join together with ecstasy and charisma in new organizations, or "movements," seeking status and function for their members.

10. *Task Specialization*

Whereas medical history provides us with good illustrations of the social process of personal specialization, the organizational process of task specialization is best illustrated by the history of the industrial worker. The industrial revolution sharply reduced the industrial worker's control over his own destiny by necessarily centralizing control over machines; and the growth in the use of machines was facilitated by the microdivision of work. Although the machine increased production enormously, it was instrumental in keeping workers docile by threatening them with displacement. The power of workers was further reduced by increased competition brought about by reduction in the num-

[1] Ibid., p. 411.

ber and complexity of the programs they were required to master, or by the loss of skill.[2]

Machines were incomplete and did not entirely replace men, for what the machines could not do, the men had to do. Man therefore became an appendage to the machine. In the designing of machines and in the planning of men's jobs in relation to them, only man's biological capacities were considered. His tastes and motivations were ignored. It was assumed that he would do anything of which he was biologically capable if he were paid enough.[3] The programs assigned to him were considered only in relation to output per unit of time; and not even the physiological costs to the workers were considered relevant, let alone the psychological and social costs.[4] The high output, therefore, was heavily subsidized by the industrial workers. Yet the welfare of the workers could be ignored because, deprived of personal specialization, they had no power. The microdivision of work could be and was autocratically imposed.

The microdivision of work, by making the goal of activity invisible, deprived work of any meaning for the individual. He was no longer engaged in a "worthwhile" task. He became alienated from his work, and at the same time his work lost its social identity. It had no meaning for significant persons beyond the immediate work group.[5] The industrial worker lost status and function.

[2] Robert K. Merton: *Social Theory and Social Structure*, rev. ed. (Glencoe, Illinois: The Free Press; 1957), p. 565.

[3] See Frederick W. Taylor: *The Principles of Scientific Management* (New York: Harper & Brothers; 1911); also S. M. Lowry, H. B. Maynard, and G. J. Stegemerten: *Time and Motion Study* (New York: McGraw-Hill Book Co.; 1940), p. 6.

[4] Friedman: op. cit. The treatment of labor as a commodity, involving as it does the attempt to get more work for less pay, is functionally related to the indestructible belief that workers are only interested in more pay for less work. See Moore: op. cit., p. 163.

[5] How should one react to a person who says he is a water smeller, cheese sprayer, heavy forger, glass breaker, bone crusher, head chiseler, robber, rustler, oyster boxer, belly soaker, pretzel twister, duster, sausage roper, kicking-machine operator, firebug, pouncer, diamond sewer, kiss setter, mop comber, mooner, moocher, mouse-trap

This loss of status and function was accompanied by the loss of "joy in work," [6] with the result that other satisfactions had to be found in higher wages, shorter hours, and in social relations at work. The use of money as a bribe to get workers to accept unsatisfactory "specialties," however, has probably resulted only in an increased interest in wages. Likewise, the various social or recreational services provided by the organization after the completion of a dull job may have made the work seem an even more distasteful hurdle to be cleared. [7] Co-operation purchased in this way is uncertain and precarious at best. Attempts by workers to establish some control over their own destiny have taken the form of unionism and resistance to technological progress, while their attitude toward the machine has been and is one of uneasy distrust.

The industrial microdivision of labor has resulted in enormous waste of skill potential and in destruction of personality. Boredom associated with underutilization is endemic in industrial society and is allegedly met by the practice of weeding out the more able workers when the labor market allows. [8] Being an appendage to a machine which can-

winder, nose tester, dimpler, bull runner, bottom whipper, jelly pumper, dilly boy, cranberry snapper, fish pitcher, pigtailer, devil tender, sweater spotter, or a jollier? See the *Dictionary of Occupational Titles*, The Department of Labor (Washington, D.C.: G.P.O.; 1960); it has over 40,000 different job titles. See Moore: op. cit., pp. 441 ff.; Merton: op. cit., p. 564; Friedman: op. cit.

[6] Friedman: op. cit.; Benjamin M. Selekman: *Labor Relations and Human Relations* (New York: McGraw-Hill Book Co.; 1947), pp. 222-24; and Abram Kardiner: *The Individual and His Society* (New York: Columbia University Press; 1939), pp. 50-6.

[7] See Moore: op. cit., pp. 233-5.

[8] See Friedman: op. cit., p. 216; see also Morris S. Viteles: *The Science of Work* (New York: W. W. Norton & Company, Inc.; 1934), pp. 329-33, who suggested "the boon of stupidity" as a solution to human problems of mechanization. Psychologists in their work on satiation have abundantly demonstrated the psychological costs of repetitive simple programs. See Gardner Lindzey, ed.: *Handbook of Social Psychology* (Reading, Massachusetts: Addison-Wesley Publishing Company, Inc.; 1954), Vol. I, ch. v. The notion of psychologically complete

not talk, the industrial worker frequently is socially isolated.[9] Friedman summarizes the human costs of the industrial microdivision of labor as follows: [1]

1. Fatigue.
2. Bad working conditions, especially noise and vibration.
3. Failure to adapt the machine to man's biopsychological nature, forcing man to adapt to the machine.
4. Accidents.
5. Monotony.
6. Loss of natural work rhythm.
7. Separation of thought and intelligence from work.
8. Degradation and reduction of skills.
9. Dehumanization from the rationalization of occupational training.

Although the industrial microdivision of labor has been enormously costly in terms of the individual welfare of the workers, it has also been enormously productive in terms of output. The reason for this apparent contradiction is that the microdivision of human labor made possible the employment of incompletely designed machines; what was lost in worker welfare was repaid in production. Since the tremendously productive machine was incomplete, little bits and parts of man had to be used to complete it. The rest of the

versus psychologically incomplete tasks leads to the same conclusions. Ibid.

[9] Some "human-relations" people now stress "satisfactory social living" in the work situation. See T. N. Whitehead: *Leadership in a Free Society* (Cambridge: Harvard University Press; 1936), ch. viii; also Elton Mayo: *Human Problems of an Industrial Civilization* (New York: The Macmillan Co.; 1933). The sociologist Reinhard Bendix believes that this objective is chimerical. He feels that the institutional and technical compulsions of modern large-scale productive enterprises are simply not compatible with a high degree of co-operation and morale on the part of industrial workers. "Bureaucracy: the Problem and its Setting," *Am. Sociol. Rev.*, Vol. XII (1947), pp. 498-502.

[1] Op. cit. The excessive costs in destruction of personality involved in the microdivision of labor have been recognized by a long line of eminent persons, among whom are the following: Adam Smith, Buret and Sismondi, Fourier, Proudhon, Marx and Engels.

man could rationally be considered as waste, in the terms of production values. As machines became less flexible and more expensive, human labor had to become more flexible so that a human adjunct could always be found to complete the machine and to keep it fully employed. Idle machines were too costly.[2]

The microdivision of labor in industry seems to have stemmed from two sources. First, there was the need to keep partially perfected and expensive machines fully occupied. Secondly, there was the desire to avoid dependence upon skilled workers; to keep workers docile by holding the threat of displacement over them and by reducing their power.

Industrial task specialization has not met the personal and social needs which have guided the social process of specialization. Aphoristically stated, while personal specialization finds an adequate place for the lowliest, task specialization in industry has found the lowliest place for even the most adequate. It has deprived the worker of control over his own destiny by increasing his competition. It has deprived him of status and function. It has blocked the development of solidarity, as witnessed by labor-management strife and other forms of industrial conflict.[3] The industrial division

[2] The completed machine, automation, will eliminate the industrial worker; it will require skilled technicians. Thus, if automation eliminates the flexibility of labor, its introduction may eventually require some rational planning and control, if the machines are to be fully employed. Note that the proportion of unskilled workers in the labor force goes down decade by decade. See Edward Gross: *Work and Society* (New York: Thomas Y. Crowell Company; 1958), pp. 60-3. For a nontechnical survey of some of the organizational and social implications of automation, see Walter Buckingham: *Automation: Its Impact on Business and People* (New York: Harper & Brothers; 1960).

[3] Durkheim regarded the industrial division of labor as abnormal and due to inequalities in the conditions of competition. He also felt that time might bring about a more harmonious equilibrium of interests. (Op. cit.) The relationship between task specialization and industrial strife is recognized in John M. Pfiffner and Frank P. Sherwood: *Administrative Organization* (Englewood Cliffs, New Jersey: Prentice-Hall, Inc.; 1960), pp. 12-13.

of labor was not the outgrowth of a social process. It was and is a planned condition imposed upon the organization by those in authority. To the traditional seat of authority, the hierarchy, we now turn our attention.

CHAPTER 4

Hierarchy

⚓

1. *Hierarchical Roles*

A HIERARCHY is a system of roles—the roles of subordination and superordination—arranged in a chain so that role 1 is subordinate to role 2; and 2 is superordinate to 1 but subordinate to 3. The chain so continues until a role is reached that is subordinate to no other role, except perhaps to a group of people such as a board of directors or an electorate.

A role is an organized pattern of behavior in accordance with the expectations of others. Social scientists often refer to the pattern of expectations as a person's social position, or the sum of his rights and duties in a particular interactional situation; and to his role as behavior appropriate to his position.

Roles are cultural items and are learned. Thus, common roles such as the roles of mother, father, son, six-year-old, etc., are transmitted from generation to generation and vary somewhat from culture to culture. They also change in time within the same culture. The roles of subordinate and superior, that is to say man-boss roles, are likewise learned cultural patterns of behavior transmitted from generation to generation. We will refer to these roles in shorthand fashion as hierarchical roles.

As Weber has shown, early hierarchical roles were usually derived from magic and superstition.[1] The rights of command and duties of obedience ascribed to these roles derived from belief in the unusual, usually magical or supernatural powers of some individual. Weber called this kind of authority "charismatic." Early tribal chiefs seem often to have developed from that original specialist, the magician.[2] Simmel has pointed out that early kings, such as David, had many superior abilities. David was an accomplished warrior, singer, and prophet.[3] The extremely rigorous training of boys who were to become war chiefs testifies to the importance the American Indians attached to technical ability in authority roles.

The *power* of command of the early charismatic leader was legitimized into the *right* of command, or, as we would say, *authority*.[4] Whereas the *position* of the charismatic leader

[1] Max Weber: *The Theory of Social and Economic Organization*, trans. A. M. Henderson and Talcott Parsons, ed. Talcott Parsons (New York: Oxford University Press, Inc.; 1947).

[2] Sir James Frazer: *The Golden Bough*, abrid. ed. (New York: The Macmillan Co.; 1940), pp. 83 ff. Until fairly modern times kings were believed to have some unusual powers, such as the power to heal certain kinds of diseases. Charles II of Britain touched almost 100,000 persons to heal scrofula during his reign. Ibid. Note the magic staff of Moses. Durkheim saw the power of the primitive chief as the power of the common conscience imputed to him by the tribe. Emile Durkheim: *The Division of Labor in Society*, trans. George Simpson (Glencoe, Illinois: The Free Press; 1952), p. 181.

[3] Georg Simmel: *Sociology*, trans. Kurt H. Wolff (Glencoe, Illinois: The Free Press; 1950), pp. 291-4, 298-300. Simmel points out that as the group gets larger, the ruler can no longer be the standard and leader of all its interests and activities. He loses to specialization his superiority in one activity after another. The position can no longer be left to the accidents of personal characteristics and must be objectified in an institutional role—as we would say, the role of superordination.

[4] We will use the now fairly well-established definition of "power" as the ability to influence a person in a somewhat predictable fashion and of "authority" as legitimate power or influence. That is to say, if A accepts an obligation to submit to the influence of B, B has authority

was confused with the *person,* in modern bureaucracy the two are at least theoretically separated; and hierarchical roles, as we understand them, emerge as independent concepts. Roles thus become items of culture in which nearly everyone receives some training. That is to say, nearly everyone in any advanced society, if assigned to a superordinate or a subordinate position, has some clear and common understanding of the behavior appropriate to the position. Advancing specialization has tended to qualify superordinate roles. In a relatively unspecialized organization the right to command is of wider scope than in the specialized. In the latter, the right may be almost as absolute, but necessarily covers a smaller area of influence.[5]

Defining position as a system of rights and duties in a situation of interaction, and role as behavior appropriate to a position, we can well turn our attention now to a discussion of the rights and duties associated with hierarchical roles.

2. *Rights and Duties*

Being cultural items, these roles tend to change in harmony with other items of the culture. In our own culture, the growth of literacy, the decline of magic and superstition, the pre-eminence of science, the beliefs associated with lib-

over A. See Herbert Goldhammer and Edward A. Shils: "Types of Power and Status," *Am. J. Sociol.,* Vol. XLV (1939), pp. 171-8. For a brief discussion of the source of hierarchical roles in the European culture, see Walter B. Miller: "Two Concepts of Authority," *The American Anthropologist* (April 1955).

[5] Note Weber's contention that obedience in bureaucratic organizations is prompt, automatic, and unquestioning. Op. cit. Weber said that in the bureaucratic organization authority was limited by a rationalized system of rules so that it was not personal but legal. The same idea is contained in the concept of the "rule of law." However, *men* always rule, not the law, although the ruler's authority in a specialized system can only be exercised within his defined competence. Hence, it is often necessary to refer to the law (the rules and regulations) to determine the extent or limit of his authority so that he will not intrude upon someone else's competence.

eralism and democracy, the rich associational life of our people—all bring pressures on the old role definitions. As we shall see in the next chapter, the advance of specialization has especially brought pressures for modification of hierarchical roles. For various reasons discussed below, they are resistant to these pressures. Nevertheless, there is some lack of consensus concerning role definitions, and so the discussion of the rights and duties associated with hierarchical roles will be somewhat controversial.

First let us consider the role of a "superior"—the superordinate role. When a person is designated as the "boss," what does this mean?[6] In the first place, it means that he has a right to veto or to affirm the organizationally directed proposals of his subordinates, subject to no appeal. Furthermore, the superior's rights include a nearly absolute veto power over the personal goals of subordinates, such as raises or promotions. Although there are many promotional arrangements, nearly all depend heavily and ultimately on the kind word from the "boss." [7] However, rights of appeal from actions affecting personal goals are beginning to appear.

Hierarchical relations overemphasize the veto and underemphasize approval of innovation. Since there is no appeal from the superior's decision, a veto usually ends the matter. However, an approval will often have to go to the next higher level where it is again subject to a veto. A hierarchical system, therefore, always favors the status quo. In a collegiate body, individual members have a free constituency to which they can appeal and get a hearing. Even in collegiate bodies, however, for example legislatures, there

[6] Note that his rights and duties are rarely specified. It is assumed that these are well understood by all. The following discussion of the hierarchical institution seems to be consistent at most points with that of Walter B. Miller (loc. cit.).

[7] See Norman J. Powell: *Personnel Administration in Government* (Englewood Cliffs, New Jersey: Prentice-Hall, Inc.; 1956), pp. 395-8. Also see Harold J. Leavitt: *Managerial Psychology* (Chicago: University of Chicago Press; 1958), pp. 259-62; and Wilbert E. Moore: *Industrial Relations and The Social Order*, rev. ed. (New York: The Macmillan Co.; 1951), p. 143.

is some hierarchy, and so the *status quo* is also favored in these bodies. The advantage is on the side of those who oppose innovations, such as new legislation; the advantage is on the side of the veto. (Here we do not refer to collegiate bodies such as a Russian Soviet, which are hierarchical creations.)

Rights of appeal from decisions affecting personal goals have only recently begun to appear in our bureaucratic organizations, although they have long existed in the state. The absence of a right of appeal from other kinds of superordinate decisions raises a problem which hierarchical institutions have never been able to solve. This is the problem of how to correct flagrant misuse of the authority of the boss's position. We have no legitimate way of solving this problem. It has sometimes been solved by mutiny. Usually it has been solved by subordinate plotting and "back-stabbing." Mutiny puts an enormous risk and responsibility upon subordinates. If they are later judged to have acted wisely (though illegally, of course), they become heroes. Otherwise, they are likely to go before a firing squad, or its bureaucratic equivalent.[8] In either case, mutiny requires heroic behavior.

The superior is generally considered to have the right to expect obedience and loyalty from his subordinates.[9] Although Weber thought that the separation of public, or organizational, rights and duties from private, or personal, rights and duties was one of the hallmarks of modern

[8] The author of the *Caine Mutiny* ruled that mutiny is immoral even if the mutineers are later exonerated. This position is widely held. It is the position of Hobbes, and is based on the assumption that conditions under a breakdown of formal authority are so bad that nothing could possibly justify considered disobedience. Less charismatically impressed, Locke concluded that a breakdown of formal authority brings only inconvenience and is much to be preferred to tyranny.

[9] Note the widespread reaction against the late Senator McCarthy's assertion that public officials owe their first loyalty to the United States, not to their bureaucratic superiors. For the same reasons there has been considerable criticism of the Nuremberg trials of war criminals because the command of a superior officer was not accepted as a defense.

bureaucracy, bureaucratic demands upon subordinates extend to many aspects of their personal lives.[1] The right to obedience is only another aspect of the right to command. It should be noted that this is the right to command autocratically and arbitrarily, as Weber indicated. Although there are many superiors who do not supervise autocratically and arbitrarily, they nevertheless have the right to do so.

The superior has the right to monopolize communication, both official communication between the unit and the outside world and communication between the members of the unit. The right to monopolize outgoing communication is often expressed by the insistence upon "going through channels" and by bitter resistance to the use of specialist, nonhierarchical channels. The right to dominate internal communication is less often pressed. In autocratically supervised units, however, communication often comes close to a one-way, star-shaped pattern—a restriction of communication to the superior-subordinate relationship only.

The superior has the right to deference from his subordinates. What makes this right significant is that it is one-way. The superior has a right to be somewhat insensitive as to subordinates' personal needs.[2] The ranking of roles with regard to the amount of deference due them is what we mean by the "status system."[3] Although specialties are also status ranked, by far the most visible and virile ranking in organization is ranking according to hierarchical position.

[1] See William H. Whyte, Jr.: *The Organization Man* (Garden City, New York: Doubleday & Company, Inc.; 1957).

[2] Moore: op. cit., pp. 183-4. He says this insensitivity of superiors to the needs of subordinates is the cause of much trouble in organizations. Harold Leavitt says superiors generally resist the introduction of objective performance standards because they interfere with the superiors' right to dominate the situation, to command respect, to rule the roost. Op. cit., p. 261.

[3] The term "status system" is not entirely adequate. "Status" is a social position. Positions are ranked according to the amount of deference due them—according to their prestige. Here we are really concerned with the "prestige system"; however, the term "status system" has been used so much in place of such terms as "prestige system" that we feel it will communicate more.

Thus, the status system of an organization corresponds very closely to the hierarchy of superior-subordinate roles. From these primary rights of the superior flow, logically, certain secondary rights: the right to determine the personnel of the unit and its organizational form; the right to initiate activities, and to set the unit's goal; the right to assign activities and to confer jurisdiction; the right to settle conflicts and to make decisions. His power of command makes it possible for him to create nonhierarchical authority by ordering his subordinates to submit to the influence of persons other than himself in various specialized areas.

The rights associated with hierarchical positions are cultural definitions. Actual behavior associated with these positions will be modified by personality, any one person being more or less authoritarian than another. More importantly, actual behavior will be modified by the social process within the groups of people which compose the organization. Thus, a superior may form strong affective attachments to his subordinates; he may identify with them. Having become their friend, so to speak, he will find he has assumed the duties of friendship, most of which are at war with his hierarchical rights and usually with his duties to his superior. In extreme cases of this kind, a specific individual may engage in almost no behavior appropriate to his hierarchical position; he may not enact his hierarchical role. It is not unusual in such a situation for a person so entrapped to be considered useless by the hierarchy and to be replaced. Perhaps most people in hierarchical positions find their roles compromised in this fashion to a greater or lesser degree.

Although hierarchical role behavior may be modified by personality or the group identification of the superior, so that any one person may be more or less authoritarian than another, the important point is that the roles, as culturally defined, are autocratic and authoritarian. Democracy does not constitute a separate tradition of hierarchical roles. It consists, among other things, of devices for checking the power of superordinate roles by other kinds of power. These roles and the corresponding status system are simply incompatible with democratic egalitarianism. People are always grateful when a person in a superordinate position exercises his rights with humanitarian restraint. "He's a regular guy." They do not feel they have a right to expect this.

Above what might be considered a market minimum, the satisfactions which the organization has to offer are distributed according to hierarchical rank. They include, in addition to money, deference, power, interesting activities and associations, inside knowledge, conveniences, etc. Because these goods are distributed according to status rank, and access to any rank is controlled by hierarchical position, these positions acquire great power even over those who might not recognize all the rights of the position as they have been outlined above. Likewise, these positions become means to personal (as opposed to organizational) ends, and as such are the objects of a constant struggle.[4]

The superordinate role is chiefly characterized by rights. If it has duties, they constitute the correlatives of subordinate rights. On the other hand, the subordinate role is chiefly characterized by duties—all those duties which constitute the correlatives of the superordinate's rights. They are the duties of obedience, of loyalty, of deference; the duty to accept a superior's veto without attempting to appeal around him. Is anything more organizationally immoral than attempting to "go around" a superior? In our modern democratic culture there are demands for rights of subordinates, rights to personal dignity, to being treated on the basis of merit, to extraorganizational freedom from organizational superiors. All of these "rights" are ambiguous because they conflict with superordinate rights, and this conflict has not yet been worked out in our culture. That is to say, the doctrines of democracy and liberalism which underlie our state have made almost no impact upon our bureaucratic organizations.[5] The

[4] See ch. v, p. 97, ft. nt. 2. For a discussion of the various psychological "goods" or advantages enjoyed by the person with superior power in a relationship, see John W. Thibaut and Harold H. Kelley: *The Social Psychology of Groups* (New York: John Wiley & Sons, Inc.; 1959), pp. 116-19.

[5] The lack of interest in this liberal tradition seems to be especially pronounced among the more scientifically-oriented students of organi-

only nonlabor-union movement in this direction has been the attempt by some personnel people to introduce into the bureaucracy rudimentary elements of procedural due process to protect the personal goals of employees. But because of the persistence of the old role definitions and the actual power of hierarchies, the assurance of procedural due process is problematical in any particular organization and more or less dependent upon the personalities or connections of the people involved. To avail oneself of such protection is to risk impossible working relations with the boss.

3. The Status System

Since a large part of the role behavior associated with hierarchical positions is concerned with deference or prestige, it would be well to take a closer look at the status system. Prestige has been defined as the invidious value of a role.[6] We have defined the status system as a hierarchy of deference ranks and seen that it corresponds to the hierarchy of subordinate-superordinate roles. Although positions can be differentiated without ranking, they are usually ranked.[7]

Since a person's hierarchical position is a matter of definition, of defined rights and duties, it should be clear at the outset that any special deference paid to the incumbent may constitute a confusion of person and role. That is to say, a person may be entitled to deference by virtue of one or more of his qualities, but his role is not one of his

---

zation. For example, Thibaut and Kelley maintain that it is simpler and more effective to have the same person maintain surveillance and apply sanctions, thereby summarily rejecting the entire historical experience of Western legal institutions. (Ibid., p. 278.) For other illustrations of this attitude see the section on "managerial social psychology" in ch. vi, below.

[6] Kingsley Davis: "A Conceptual Analysis of Stratification," *Am. Sociol. Rev.*, Vol. VII (1942), pp. 309-21.

[7] Robert K. Merton: *Social Theory and Social Structure*, rev. ed. (Glencoe, Illinois: The Free Press; 1957), p. 315.

qualities. However, a person is perceived by others through his roles, his public or perceived personality being the sum of his various roles.[8]

The confusion of office, or role, and person is a very old phenomenon.[9] It was part of the charismatic pattern. In fact, status can be regarded as the continuation of charismatic attitudes and practices. People impute superior abilities to persons of higher status,[1] and this imputed superior ability is generalized into a halo of superiority. Persons of very high status, therefore, are called upon to help solve problems of every conceivable kind—problems about which they could have no knowledge whatsoever. In public affairs, this halo effect of status requires high-status persons to speak out on all sorts of matters from a position of almost complete ignorance. They are, therefore, forced to develop

[8] G. H. Mead: *Mind, Self, and Society* (Chicago: University of Chicago Press; 1934); Theodore R. Sarbin: "Role Theory," in Gardner Lindzey, ed.: *Handbook of Social Psychology* (Reading, Massachusetts: Addison-Wesley Publishing Company, Inc.; 1954); Kingsley Davis: loc. cit.

[9] The history of diplomacy is especially rich in illustrations of excessive concern with the symbols of rank. In early times, the symbols of status or rank were partly a mechanical approach to maintaining the charisma of an earlier leader. Fights over rank often amounted to neurotic insistence upon the "charisma" or "unusual characteristics" of what was usually an ordinary or less than ordinary man. As Weber said, his retainers were interested in maintaining his "charisma" by any means, because that was how they protected their own special privileges, including wealth and power. Weber: op. cit. See Thorstein Kalijarvi and Associates: *Modern World Politics*, 3rd ed. (New York: Thomas Y. Crowell Company; 1954), pp. 221-2; and R. B. Mowat: *A History of European Diplomacy, 1451-1789* (New York: Longmans, Green & Co., Inc.; 1928), especially p. 187. Durkheim said that the power of the primitive tribe was symbolized by the position of the chief but finally came to be imputed to the person of the chief. "The properly professional services which the [chief] renders are little things in comparison with the extraordinary power with which he is invested." Durkheim: op. cit., pp. 180-1.

[1] See Chester Barnard: "Functions and Pathology of Status Systems in Formal Organizations," in William Foote Whyte, ed.: *Industry and Society* (New York: McGraw-Hill Book Co.; 1946).

plausible-sounding jargons and propositions which come to constitute pseudo-technologies in terms of which many of our public problems must be publicly analyzed and discussed.[2] If, with this handicap, real solutions are found to these problems, they are found by unsung "staff" specialists who must perforce solve the problems in ways which do not jolt the pseudo-technologies too profoundly.

It has already been pointed out that status has a dominant position in the distributive system. Studies with small groups show that high-status persons get the most satisfactions from such groups.[3] Studies of military behavior suggest that high-status persons are more interested in preserving the system of status ranking than are low-status persons.[4] Above a certain level it would seem that salaries are to some rather large extent a function of status—the higher the status, the higher the salary. In fact, it would seem that salaries operate chiefly as symbols of status rank.[5] That the perquisites and conveniences of the work situation are distributed according to status rather than organizational need is common knowledge, and it has been argued that they are distributed in inverse ratio to need.[6] These perquisites also

[2] See Cecil A. Gibb: "Leadership," in Gardner Lindzey, ed.: op. cit., p. 905. See also Norton E. Long: "The Local Community as an Ecology of Games," *Am. J. Sociol.*, Vol. LXIV (1958), pp. 251-61. The pressure upon high-status people to speak out plausibly on a great range of subjects has given rise to a new and highly paid profession—the ghost writers. See Daniel M. Burham: "Corporate Ghosts," *The Wall Street Journal* (January 4, 1960), p. 1.

[3] Robert F. Bales: "The Equilibrium Problem in Small Groups," in Talcott Parsons, Robert F. Bales, and Edward A. Shils: *Working Papers in The Theory of Action* (Glencoe, Illinois: The Free Press; 1953).

[4] Samuel Stouffer, et al.: *The American Soldier*, Vol. I (Princeton, New Jersey: Princeton University Press; 1949), pp. 391 ff.

[5] See Moore: op. cit., p. 125. George Thomas Washington and V. Henry Rothschild, in *Compensating the Corporation Executive* (New York: The Ronald Press Company; 1951), do a good job of refuting arguments that the existing pattern of executive compensation has a purely utilitarian function in relation to organization goals.

[6] Fritz Roethlisberger: *Management and Morale* (Cambridge: Harvard University Press; 1941), p. 77; and Victor A. Thompson: *The*

act as symbols, and, along with other symbols such as salaries, methods of payment, clothing, insignia, titles, etc., help to maintain the status system by increasing its visibility.[7] The amount of deference a person receives is made manifest by the good things others give him; and so, in one sense, the status system *is* the distributive system.

We have said that a hierarchical position carries with it rights to a certain amount of deference. However, the system of deference ranking, the status system, while it corresponds to the hierarchical system, is much more than a hierarchy of deference rights. These rights are owed by a group of subordinates, but a person's status spreads its influence over a much broader area. Furthermore, the amount of prestige attached to hierarchical positions increases at a striking rate as we go up the hierarchy. The status system appears to have a quasi-neurotic character.[8] This element of exaggeration in status systems has both structural and psychological determinants.

Cognitive stability is promoted if one's superior by definition is perceived as one's superior in abilities.[9] The subordinate's self-image is protected by the same mechanism.[1] The superordinate position and the person who occupies it are perceptually merged.

Regulatory Process in OPA Rationing (New York: King's Crown Press; 1950).

[7] See Barnard: loc. cit. See also Thibaut and Kelley. They equate the status system with the distributive system. Op. cit., ch. xii.

[8] With regard to the military status system, Ralph H. Turner says: "However, through their charisma officers are generally held in far greater awe than their actual powers or inclinations warrant, and a lesser officer is often afraid even to suggest to a superior that his request is not in keeping with regulations." From "The Navy Disbursing Officer," *Am. Sociol. Rev.*, Vol. XII (1947), pp. 342-8.

[9] See works by Fritz Heider, for example, "Social Perception and Phenomenal Causality," *Psychol. Rev.*, Vol. LI (1944), pp. 358-74.

[1] Barnard: op. cit. The difficulties encountered when orders must be taken from persons perceived as having lower status are well illustrated by interpersonal problems of chefs and waitresses. See William Foote Whyte: *Human Relations in the Restaurant Industry* (New York: McGraw-Hill Book Co.; 1948).

The superior's restriction of the subordinate's freedom and his power to frustrate the subordinate's ambitions result in hostilities. The hostilities are not compatible with acts of submission, and they create guilt. Consequently, according to Erich Fromm, they are suppressed and replaced by admiration.[2] My superior is wonderful, and I neither need to be ashamed of submission to him nor need I try to be equal to him in any way. If Fromm is correct, hierarchical status may be partly a result of "reaction formation."

Furthermore, the person as perceived by others is the result of his many roles. His prestige relates to the perception of his roles. Prestige is more easily maintained when there is considerable vagueness about a person's roles; about what he actually does. On the other hand, a person whose prestige is based on what he actually can do must constantly struggle to maintain it.[3] That is to say, charismatic status rank, being mysterious to the observer, is both surer and more general than status rank based upon a specialty. Incumbents of high office are held in awe because they are in touch with the mysteries and magic of such office; they are "on the inside," [4] have "inside information," etc. Since one knows less and less about the activities of superordinates the farther away in the hierarchy they are, the greater is the awe in which he holds them, and consequently the greater is their prestige or status. It is difficult, for example, for workers to impute superior qualities to their foremen, because they know fairly well what the foremen do, both at work and away from work. The same is not true for the

[2] *Escape From Freedom* (New York: Holt, Rinehart and Winston, Inc.; 1941), pp. 165-6. On the ambivalence generated by the authority relationship, see also Gardner Murphy: *Personality* (New York: Harper & Brothers; 1947), pp. 845-6; and David Krech and Richard S. Crutchfield: *Theory and Problems of Social Psychology* (New York: McGraw-Hill Book Co.; 1948), p. 421.

[3] See Norman Miller: "The Jewish Leadership of Lakeport," in Alvin W. Gouldner, ed.: *Studies in Leadership: Leadership and Democratic Action* (New York: Harper & Brothers; 1950), pp. 206-7.

[4] Phillip Selznick: "An Approach to a Theory of Bureaucracy," *Am. Sociol. Rev.,* Vol. VIII (1943).

men higher up.[5] In this sense, status rank is a function of ignorance. The hierarchy is a highly restricted system of communication, with much information coming in to each position; but the amount sent out to subordinates is subject to the control of the incumbent and for strategic or other reasons is always limited. There results an increasing vagueness as to the activities at each level as one mounts the hierarchy, and this vagueness supports the prestige ranking which we call the status system.[6]

Experimental studies with small groups indicate that stratification, or invidious ranking, in such groups is positively correlated with leader dominance behavior and negatively correlated with leader membership behavior.[7] Hierarchical roles are simply institutionalized dominance. The status system is thus seen as inseparable from the hierarchy. Furthermore, groups seem to have a process or mechanism similar to *homeostasis* in biology. If one member of the group engages in tension-producing behavior, the others act so as to reduce tension.[8] Thus if the rights of deference are pushed by a group's superior, if he "pulls rank," tensions may be reduced by acceding to the superior's demands. Communication blockages between the superior and the group reduce its influence over him so that the group must usually adjust to the superior, rather than the reverse. Supporting this deference-building process is the cultural norm in our society that a person's presentation of himself should be taken at face value.[9] The role relations between superior and subordinates, therefore, create a situation where there is almost no limit to the expansion of the superior's prestige except the prestige rank of the superior at the next level.

[5] See Henri De Man: *Joy in Work*, trans. Eden and Cedar Paul (London: George Allen and Unwin, Ltd.; 1929), pp. 200-4.

[6] Gouldner has pointed out that studies of organizations, financed as they are by management, are not allowed to pry into the activities of the higher status hierarchical positions. Op. cit., p. 48.

[7] Cecil A. Gibb: loc. cit., p. 899.

[8] Ibid., p. 901.

[9] See Erving Goffman: *The Presentation of Self in Everyday Life* (Garden City, New York: Doubleday & Company, Inc.; 1959).

People vary greatly in their needs for dominance and for status. One would expect a sort of natural selection to bring into hierarchies persons with great dominance and status needs. Persons whose dominance needs are satisfied by mastery over materials rather than people will probably become specialists of some kind. Others may satisfy their dominance needs by identifying with their organization superior, thereby reinforcing his drive to dominance and status. Whereas specialists are always subordinate, a hierarchical position always includes a superordinate role and hence a chance to dominate people.[1] Given the group adjustment mechanism of "homeostasis" and a natural selection of people with great status and dominance needs, the exaggerated character of the status system becomes intelligible, since people with great status needs can get just about as much deference as they demand if they occupy hierarchical positions.

It has often been noted that there are few operational performance standards for hierarchical positions.[2] Incumbents can never be sure "how well they are doing." Their activities have less and less of specialist content and become more and more purely hierarchical role playing.[3] What specialist content remains at very high levels relates only to the particular organization an incumbent is in and has to do mostly with its history, its organization and methods, and the idiosyncrasies of some of its personnel, clients, or suppliers. As one goes up the hierarchy, therefore, he has less

[1] According to Erich Fromm, this fact contributed much to the Nazis' success in Germany. Op. cit., ch. vi, especially pp. 236-7. The elaborate Nazi hierarchy provided opportunities for domination and submission for many authoritarian personalities with their combination of sadistic and masochistic characteristics.

[2] Moore: op. cit., p. 143; also James G. March and Herbert A. Simon: *Organizations* (New York: John Wiley & Sons, Inc.; 1958). p. 63. Of course, a particular office may include specialist as well as hierarchical activities, and operational performance standards for the former may be available.

[3] This loss of functions to specialists has been noted by many writers. See, for example, Leavitt: op. cit., pp. 238, 266, 269; and Moore: op. cit., p. 76.

and less value for other organizations.[4] These two conditions —lack of operational performance standards and lack of opportunities in other organizations—make for great anxiety. This anxiety is most likely to express itself in a neurotic overemphasis on pleasing the boss, which serves only to increase the boss's self-evaluation and therefore his demands for deference.

Prolonged enactment of a role reacts upon the personality.[5] People become what they do. The deference accorded a person who performs a hierarchical role gradually modifies his self-characterization and therefore his self-projection. He comes to feel that the deference is due him by right, that he truly is a superior person; and the deference system is further inflated.

The inflation at the upper end of the status system results in a deflation at lower levels. Since the status system controls distribution, the organization gives a great deal at the top and very little at the bottom.[6] It has often been observed that at the middle and lower-middle reaches of the hierarchy, concern with status and with the symbols of status reaches an almost pathological intensity.[7] At these points people with great dominance and status needs find less than enough to satisfy their needs because so much has been allocated to the positions above. The status system is a skewed distribution system.

4. Charisma and The Monistic Formulation

We have shown that hierarchical roles, as culturally defined, have strong charismatic elements connected with them.

[4] See March and Simon: op. cit., p. 102.

[5] Merton: "Bureaucratic Structure and Personality," op. cit., ch. vi. See also Willard Waller: *The Sociology of Teaching* (New York: John Wiley & Sons, Inc.; 1932).

[6] See Barnard: loc. cit.

[7] Moore: op. cit.; Carl Dreyfuss: *Occupation and Ideology of the Salaried Employee*, trans. Ernst E. Warbling (New York: Columbia University Press; 1938).

Current conceptions of organization are clearly based upon charismatic assumptions concerning these roles. It will be recalled that current formulations of bureaucratic organization, which we have called "monistic," and Weber "mono-cratic," conceptualize organization entirely in terms of hierarchy, as follows:

1. The person in each hierarchical position is told what to do by the person in the hierarchical position above him, and by no one else. He in turn, and he alone, tells his subordinates what to do. They, and they alone, do the same for their subordinates. These instructions establish the division of work, namely the organization. The authority to do anything is cascaded down in this way, and only in this way, by the process of delegation.

2. Each subordinate is guided (supervised or directed) in carrying out these instructions by his superior and no one else, who, in turn, is guided in this guiding by his superior and no one else, etc.

3. Each superior "controls" his subordinates in carrying out the instructions by holding them responsible for compliance with the instructions or with performance standards associated with them. The subordinates are responsible to their superior, and no one else; he, in turn, is responsible to his superior and no one else; etc. Thus, all authority comes from the top and is cascaded down by progressive delegations, while responsibility comes from the bottom and is owed to the next superior and to no one else.[8]

This monistic formulation is based upon charismatic as-

[8] For examples of this monistic concept in current organization theory see: Mary Cushing Howard Niles: *Middle Management* (New York: Harper & Brothers; 1941); Marshall E. Dimock: *The Executive in Action* (New York: Harper & Brothers; 1945); L. C. Marshall: *Business Administration* (Chicago: University of Chicago Press; 1921); Paul E. Holden, Lounsberry S. Fish, and Hubert L. Smith: *Top Management Organization and Control* (Stanford: Stanford University Press; 1941); The First Hoover Commission Report (Washington, D.C.: G.P.O.; 1949).

sumptions at various points. These assumptions will be extensively analyzed in later chapters, but it will be helpful to indicate them briefly at this point. It is assumed that the superior, at any point in the hierarchy, is *able* to tell his subordinates what to do, and to guide them in doing it. That is, it is assumed that he is more capable in all of his unit's activities than any of his subordinate specialists who perform them. As will be discussed later, the concept of responsibility for results assumes the ability or capacity to determine the results. Otherwise the responsibility is merely ritualistic. The concept of unity of command or influence denies the relevance of the nonhierarchical expertise within the organization; the hierarchy of subordinate-superior roles, the "line of command," is sufficient. When these assumptions of superordinate ability are viewed against the background of the increasing range of activities subordinate to hierarchical positions at successively higher stages in modern bureaucracy, the assumptions clearly leave the realm of objective reality and become charismatic.

5. *Nonhierarchical Authority and The Monistic Formulation*

We have been discussing hierarchical authority relationships —the relationships of boss and men. But there is also nonhierarchical authority in bureaucracy. The superior's right of command makes it possible for him to command his subordinates to obey the commands of another person in some restricted area of activities. He can *delegate* authority, by which we mean that he can create it. Nonhierarchical authority is a creation of the organization, shaped and limited according to its needs. It is, consequently, defined and specific. It is, in effect, a quality conferred upon a specialized function which defines the degree of finality of the function. Consequently, nonhierarchical authority can be withdrawn from a position without destroying its function. For example, it is possible to have a formally advisory personnel branch without destroying the personnel function.

If the contributions of a specialty are technically necessary for the accomplishment of an organization's goal, acceptance or rejection of these contributions cannot be made a right of persons outside of this specialty. With the advance of science and technology, more and more specialties are of this kind. In modern organizations, therefore, an individual finds himself subject to the authority of his boss, and, in addition, to the nonhierarchical authority of many specialized jurisdictions throughout the organization. This situation violates the monocratic institution of hierarchy with its expectation of unity of command. "No man can serve two masters." Even if nonhierarchical authority is not *formally* conferred upon a technically *necessary* specialty, the specialty will acquire unofficial power or influence.

Because nonhierarchical authority is hierarchically created, it is always subject to a formal right of appeal. What one has the right to give, he has the right to take away. An official who dislikes an order from a colleague exercising nonhierarchical authority over him has the right to appeal the order to their common boss. This right of appeal helps to meliorate this violation of monocratic expectations. However, the prevailing informal power relationships may make this right of appeal a thing of little importance. The person attempting to appeal an act of nonhierarchical authority, say a decision of Central Purchasing, will not likely find the high-level common superior receptive to many such appeals. The former will often need to persuade a reluctant superior to make the appeal for him; and in any case, his future dependence upon the nonhierarchical authority position counsels him to maintain cordial relations with the incumbent. In this case, as in so many others, the formal right tends to disappear in the realities of dynamic, informal, power relationships.

To summarize, nonhierarchical authority differs from hierarchical authority in the following ways: (1) it is more specific; (2) it relates to organizational rather than to personal goals; (3) it can be withdrawn without destroying the position; (4) it is organizationally rather than culturally defined—peculiar to the organization rather than to the culture; and (5) it is always subject to formal appeal.

6. Inadequacy of The Monistic Formulation

The monistic concept is unable to account for specialization. More specifically, it cannot account for the delegation of nonhierarchical authority. The existence of such authority is consequently denied or hidden by fictions, as, for example, "The staff only advises; it does not command." Furthermore, the monistic concept asserts that *hierarchical authority* is created by delegation from above. We have seen, on the contrary, that it is a cultural phenomenon, compounded from the culturally derived roles of the superior and the subordinate. Only nonhierarchical authority is created by delegation from above.

The monistic concept, since it is based entirely upon the institution of hierarchy and completely ignores the fact of specialization, naturally confuses rights with abilities: for example, the right to make decisions with the ability to do so. This confusion of rights with abilities results in the popular journalistic presentation of the actions of organizations, including states, as the actions of their top officials. It also encourages elitist interpretations of society, one of the latest of which is *The Power Elite* by C. Wright Mills.[9]

Hierarchical roles began to develop at times and under conditions when it was credible to think of the chief as the most capable person. Under these circumstances, vast rights became associated with the role. Belief in the unusual powers, or charisma, of persons who perform such roles has continued in the form of the status system. Although specialization has enormously changed the circumstances of organized action, modern organization theory and, to a con-

---

[9] (New York: Oxford University Press, Inc.; 1957.) His "elite" consists, by definition, of the top two or three persons in big-business, political, and military hierarchies. He says that if the line were lowered, the "elite" could be defined away (p. 18).

siderable extent, practice is fixated on the system of hierarchical roles.[1] The fact and implications of specialization
are hardly recognized in organization theory. The forcing
of specialization into the hierarchical framework gives us
our characteristic form of organization, bureaucracy. As we
shall see in the following chapters, much of the behavior
within bureaucracy derives from tensions generated by the
conflict between specialization and hierarchy. The cultural
definitions which comprise hierarchy change much more
slowly than do the facts of specialization. This resistance to
further rationalization of organized activity performs no particular instrumental function.[2] It is more in the nature of a
"cultural lag." This lag in modification of the roles is undoubtedly reinforced by vested interests in the old role
definitions because of their intimate relation to the distributive system. The lag is also reinforced by mechanisms supportive of the status system. Incompatibilities between hierarchical claims to dominance, on the one hand, and on the
other, the cultural norms of autonomy, independence, and
equality may be softened by charismatic overevaluations of
superordinates and by the other mechanisms discussed above.
Romanticism comes to the rescue of an unsatisfactory reality.

[1] Even the departmentalists, the "Gulick school," were concerned
only with arranging jobs for purposes of supervision. The jobs—
specialization—were taken for granted.

[2] Among those who have argued that the extreme deference ranking (status) aspect of these roles performs no organizational function
are Moore: op. cit., p. 138; Carl Dreyfuss: op. cit., pp. 1-18; Henri
De Man: op. cit., pp. 200-4. Barnard argues that *status* aids in communication, but he really means *positions* and *roles* rather than prestige
ranking. His point that status, as the principal motivation in organizations, is an extremely important part of the incentive system, while
true, proves too much. If status is to function as an incentive, it must
be available to all. The skewed distribution of status causes it to act as
an anti-incentive; it reduces solidarity, hence motivation to co-operate.
Barnard himself points this out. (Loc. cit.) See also Moore: op. cit.,
p. 184; Peter Drucker: *The New Society: The Anatomy of the Industrial Order* (New York: Harper & Brothers; 1950), pp. 92-5.

7. The Nature of Monocratic Institutions

In a monocratic institution only one claim, value, or course of action is proper or legitimate in any particular situation. Such institutions, therefore, are not committed to the provision of arrangements for effecting compromises. A pluralistic institution, on the other hand, accepts the legitimacy of conflict, the legitimacy of conflicting claims or proposals for action, and for that reason must provide procedures for effecting compromises. In Russia, for example, only action consistent with the historical destiny of the proletariat is legitimate; and the ability to detect this destiny by reading from the laws of history is presumed to be concentrated in the Communist Party. Therefore, no compromising or bargaining procedures can be recognized or given official blessing. In our society, on the contrary, based as it is on individual and group rights, many institutional arrangements for effecting compromises must be provided, such as parties and elections, industrial arbitration, and labor-management negotiations. Of course, wherever people work together compromises must in fact be reached. In the monocratic institution, they are reached extra-legally, or "informally"; in the pluralistic institution they are reached through formal, official, recognized devices. Thus, labor-management bargaining takes place in Russia, but not through institutionalized channels. A pluralistic institution reaches single conclusions by compromise between rightful claimants. A monocratic institution in fact reaches compromises, but the obligation to do so cannot be admitted.

On the informal side, institutions tend to be much the same, or different only in degree, because they use the same basic materials—that is, they deal with human beings. On the formal side, institutions may differ radically in kind or quality, as do monocratic and pluralistic institutions. Thus, for example, Russia and the United States are not to be distinguished from one another by citing statistics of production, births, deaths, income, delinquency, crime, treatment of minorities, education, elections, etc., but by the institutional or moral ideas behind them. The important difference is between the formal structures, not the informal behaviors of the two peoples. The United States is formally pluralistic; Russia is formally monocratic. The distinction between formal structure and informal behavior is basic for clarity of thought about many problems.

CHAPTER 5

Conflict

꧅

1. Universalism versus Particularism in Bureaucracy

IN THIS CHAPTER we shall study the interactions between specialist and hierarchical roles and the kind of order resulting. The behavior of people in organizations is purposive in two senses. First, behavior must be minimally oriented to a common organizational purpose, or it would not be meaningful to speak of an organization. Secondly, behavior within organizations is oriented to personal goals. We are interested, therefore, in role interaction in the promotion of organization goals and in the pursuit of personal goals. The first interest stresses capacities, abilities, powers; while the second stresses motivation.

Activities and relationships oriented to the objective, externalized goals of the organization stress *instrumental* considerations. That is to say, these activities and relationships are judged chiefly by their effectiveness in promoting the organization's goals rather than the personal goals of participants. The questions asked of them are rational and technical; underlying them are science and technology. These activities and relationships are definite and specific. They reflect the advance of knowledge and technique. Consequently, they reflect the advance of specialization. Scientific and technological principles are universal rather than particularistic. They are not valid for only a particular class, nation, religion, or what not. Consequently, the *instrumental elements* of organizational experience depend upon an institutional environment which encourages rationalism and universalism. This is the environment of modern, "enlightened," industrialized countries—the countries where science and technology are most advanced and bureaucracy is most developed.

On the other hand, the relationships most closely associated with personal goals in our bureaucratic structures stress *rights* or *authority* rather than instrumental considerations. These relationships tend to be diffuse rather than specific, and particularistic rather than universal. They are the relationships of hierarchy. The subordinate is dependent upon the superior for many important personal goals. At the same time, objective standards governing the relationship, such as bills of rights, are lacking. "Merit" itself is essentially a subjective judgment. The subordinate's obligations to his superior, therefore, tend to be ill-defined and diffuse rather than definite and specific. In the absence of objective and universal criteria governing this relationship, particularistic norms take their place, such as personal connections, appearance, mannerisms, dress, family relationship, social class, race, religion, nationality, college affiliation, and others the reader can supply for himself. To realize his personal goals in the organization, the subordinate has to please the boss, whatever this requires. Technical competence is not enough.

Within modern organizations, therefore, we see one pattern in which activities and relationships are carefully defined and governed by the universalism of modern science and technology. We see another pattern in which relationships are ill-defined and only vaguely limited, are diffuse rather than specific, and in which particularism is the dominant criterion.[1] The first pattern is new; the second, old. Bureaucracy, again, is seen to be compounded of the new and the old, of specialization and hierarchy.

2. Factoring and The Delegation of Jurisdiction

In a preceding chapter we defined a specialist as a person skilled in a number of specific programs—fairly complex sets of organized activities of a practical nature. As problem-solving mechanisms, organizations can be viewed as a breaking down, or factoring, of a general problem into simpler and more specific sets of activities until actual programs are reached. This general problem is the accomplishment of the organizational goal. New problems for an existing organization are similarly factored. Such factoring creates the general structure of the organization. Although determining the structure of the organization is a *right* of the superior, as we saw in the last chapter, he has lost the *ability* to do the job because of growing complexity. New specialists in organization have appeared who do part of the job. For the most part, however, the way to factor a problem is indicated by the technologies required to achieve the goal of the organization. It is largely determined by the process of specialization. To the extent that rational decisions are required to complete this factoring they will be for the most part the decisions of a group of technical specialists, because most of the questions involved are technical, having to do with the instrumental relations between the organization's structure and its goals. If *other* than instrumental considerations are taken into account, however, the superior will be involved in the factoring. For example, the person with the right to make such a decision may have non-technical, possibly personal, reasons for centralizing some

[1] See Peter B. Hammond: "The Functions of Indirection in Communication," in *Comparative Studies in Administration*, edited by the Staff of the Administrative Science Center, University of Pittsburgh (University of Pittsburgh Press; 1959). See also Talcott Parsons: *Essays in Sociological Theory Pure and Applied* (Glencoe, Illinois: The Free Press; 1949), ch. viii.

activity at a level beyond what is technically necessary. (See ch. iii.)

Associated with the factoring of the organization's goal is the delegation of jurisdictions, that is to say, the creation of nonhierarchical authority relationships. In the previous chapter we described the hierarchical system, which is the principal system of authority in organizations. The authority relationships of hierarchy are the relationships of superior to subordinate. The superior's right to command, however, makes it possible for him to create by delegation nonhierarchical authority relationships. He can command his subordinates to accede to the influence of another person in some defined area or specialty. He can, therefore, centralize activities or create interdependencies. Since this power of a superior is not necessarily restricted by any formula or operational standard, it is essentially political power, that is to say, the personal power to confer favors. To the extent that it is exercised apart from any operational standard, the process which activates it is a political process. The existence of such a power creates bureaucratic politics. But to the extent that this power is exercised in accordance with the needs of specialization, it constitutes a *pro forma* legitimizing of technical reality, an official promulgation of technically existing interdependence.

The making of work assignments is almost universally designated as an "executive function." However, most behavior in bureaucratic organizations is programmed. These programs are rarely activated by the commands of a superior, although he may serve as a channel of communication. They are activated by incoming information or by executed programs from other parts of the organization which reach the individual through the proceduralized flow of work. Only rarely are new programs or innovation needed. Although legitimizing innovations is a superordinate right, *innovation* is very much a *specialist function*, not only because new programs come from specialist organizations and educational curricula, but also because they are suggested by the interpretation of incoming raw data, an activity which of necessity is specialized. The approval of innovations is most likely based upon confidence in their sources and the order of their appearance.[2] If approval is based upon the technical adequacy of the proposal, necessarily a specialist determination, the *right* of approval becomes a formality only.

The right to approve new organizational *goals*, as well as programs, is a superordinate right.[3] However, what new goals an organization is *able* to undertake is a technical or specialist question, as is the question of whether specific alternatives will achieve given goals. Alternatives are considered factually (Will they achieve specified goals?) and from the standpoint of values (Are the goals worth achieving?). In the event of a dispute as to values, a choice must be made which is based upon confidence in one of the disputants, or upon the personal preferences of the approver. Because of the risk of the latter basis of choice, one suspects that *redefinition* of organization goals is nonhierarchical; that it is generated internally, or that it results from severe external pressures of various power structures. At the lower end of the hierarchy, the supervisor's position is more specialized in nature, sometimes highly so. If such is the case, his approval of innovations is probably based upon his evaluation of their utility. If so, he is acting in his specialist role as the one who has the most relevant knowledge or skill, rather than in his authority role as the one with most rights concerning the matter.[4]

[2] See James G. March and Herbert A. Simon: *Organizations* (New York: John Wiley & Sons, Inc.; 1958), p. 188; also Victor A. Thompson: *The Regulatory Process in OPA Rationing* (New York: King's Crown Press; 1950), pp. 303 ff.

[3] It is theoretically incorrect to say that the function of the executive is to set the goals or determine the ends of the organization. It *is* correct to say he has the right to do so as part of his superordinate role. If he exercises this right, his action will be regarded as a function by those who agree with the goals so set but not by those who disagree. Thus, to seek "*the* functions of *the* executive" is theoretically absurd, although it is theoretically proper to hypothesize about the function of the superordinate role in relation to organizations, about the functions (or dysfunctions) of the rights of which that role is composed.

[4] See ch. viii, p. 163, ft. nt. 5.

3. *Achieving Organizational Goals*

The adequacy of problem-solving within organizations depends upon the adequacy of communication as well as upon the skills available. We have already pointed out that the interdependence of specialists is made more tolerable if communication between them is adequate, and this fact encourages the development of specialized languages and useful shorthand categories for classifying large amounts of information. The relation between adequate and reliable communication on the one hand, and the tolerance of interdependence on the other, also exerts pressures for the creation of specialist communication channels beyond the formal channel of the hierarchy. Not only are the formal channels intolerably overloaded as a result of specialization, but they are now also technically inadequate for much of the communication they are called upon to carry. Furthermore, these channels are notoriously unreliable because of opportunities and motives for suppression and censorship at each hierarchical communication station. Most problem-solving communication, consequently, takes place through specialist communication channels. For reasons discussed in later chapters, these communication channels are generally not officially recognized and legitimized by organizational hierarchies. As a result, most problem-solving communication is "illegal" and surreptitious, and protected from official notice by means of myths and fictions.[5]

Since problem solving in organizations is a specialist activity, it is a group rather than an individual activity. A decision by a group of specialists must be almost unanimous; and modern organizations try to make decisions about organizational goals by unanimous groups.[6] In matters involv-

[5] See ch. vii below.
[6] See Wilbert E. Moore: *Industrial Relations and the Social Order*, rev. ed. (New York: The Macmillan Co.; 1951), p. 124, ft. nt. 14; March and Simon: op. cit., p. 118; Robert A. Gordon: *Business Leadership in the Large Corporation* (Washington, D.C.: The Brookings Institution;

ing the personal goals and ambitions of employees, however, autocratic hierarchical decision is still the rule. Although group decision is an inevitable result of specialization and interdependence, it is also a result of the recognized need for group decision. There may be, therefore, more group consultation in modern bureaucratic organizations than the objective facts of interdependence warrant.[7] This overworking of group processes, the exaggeration of interdependence, appears to result from conditions within the hierarchy rather than from specialization.[8] Since the hierarchy, by definition, is an allocation of rights rather than abilities, this emphasis on the right to be consulted, the right to review, is understandable. The relation of the hierarchical role to the decisional process is a relation of right, that is to say, of competency or jurisdiction. "Has everyone with a legitimate interest been consulted?"

Furthermore, the more joint decision is engaged in, the more the immediate superior will be called upon to settle differences, and hence the greater his influence will be. When only single recommendations can reach him, he becomes largely a captive of his organization. It is not surprising, therefore, that the superior will see the need for joint decision whether it exists or not, and that he may be tempted to create technically unnecessary interdependence by delegating authority in defiance of the needs of specialization. However, in addition to the right to be consulted, and the desire for enhanced influence, excessive insistence upon joint decision reflects the insecurity which is inherent in the position of the modern executive. This insecurity is a result of the increasing dependence upon specialists, a dependence which increases generally as special-

---

1945), pp. 99 ff.; William H. Whyte, Jr.: *The Organization Man* (Garden City, New York: Doubleday & Company, Inc.; 1957). Consultants are probably brought in because unanimity cannot be obtained. Moore: op. cit.

[7] Note Whyte's complaints on this score. Op. cit.

[8] March and Simon say that the felt need for joint decision increases as one goes up the hierarchy. They feel that since the chief legitimation of hierarchy is co-ordination, the hierarchy is likely to see the need for co-ordination whether or not it exists. Op. cit., p. 124.

ization advances, and in any particular organization as one
rises to higher position.

Problem solving by a group should generally be superior
to individual problem solving, providing the group is not
formally structured into the roles of superior and subordinates. The group provides a constant evaluation of the
thinking process as it evolves. From the reactions of others,
the thinker is constantly made aware of weaknesses and
strengths in his analysis. Inherent weaknesses in individual
problem solving, such as affective attachments to one's own
ideas, are constantly exposed. The group provides "periph-
eral vision" so badly lacking in individual problem solving
with its straight-line approach. Kelley and Thibaut summarize
the reasons for the superiority of group thinking as follows:
(1) errors are scattered, therefore their influence is reduced;
(2) considered opinions have greater influence on group
members than offhand judgments; (3) opinions expressed
confidently will have more influence, and they are more
likely to be correct; (4) group members can specialize in
aspects of the problem; (5) the group as a whole will have
more possible solutions; (6) the need to communicate forces
group members to sharpen and clarify their ideas. In addition, the group environment may increase (or decrease) motivation toward task completion, and it will motivate toward
an eventual consensus.[9]

Although group decision can be greatly superior to individual decision as a problem-solving device, bureaucratic

[9] "Experimental Studies of Group Problem Solving Process," in
Gardner Lindzey, ed.: *Handbook of Social Psychology* (Reading, Massachusetts: Addison-Wesley Publishing Company, Inc.; 1954), Vol. II.
    Since the ability to evaluate the correctness of proposed solutions
is apparently more widespread than the ability to suggest them, group
problem solving should have a better record of success than the individual problem solving. See E. L. Thorndike: "The Effect of Discussion upon the Correctness of Group Decisions when the Factor of
Majority Influence is Allowed For," *J. Soc. Psychol.*, Vol. IX (1938),
pp. 343-62.
    Whyte (op. cit.) deplores the extensive use of the group process
in formal organization, but he is referring to the formally structured
group which operates in a very different manner, as we describe below.

structure severely limits the effectiveness of the group process. For the thinking process of a small group to be most effective, a substantial degree of cohesion among members is required. This cohesion greatly increases the ability of the group members to accept and affectively to back up one another's analyses and suggestions.[1] Cohesion minimizes autocratic procedures and behavior which create tensions, dry up spontaneity and creativity, and attack co-operativeness.[2] Although many spontaneous, nonhierarchical, informal group discussions constantly take place in organizations, the decisions which commit the organization, the official decisions, take place in hierarchically structured groups. Though attempts are often made to hide the hierarchical structure in the formal group-decision process and to pretend that it is not there,[3] the hierarchy is *in fact* present and all group participants know it. Consequently, because of hierarchical control over personal goals, everything said and done in the group situation must be evaluated not only from the standpoint of its relation to the organization's goals but also from its relation to personal goals. In bureaucracy, ideas do not stand on their merits alone.[4] It is not only an opinion or an idea that wins, but also a man. The situation is inherently competitive rather than co-operative; and, as Kurt Lewin pointed out, competition attacks group solidarity and consequently the ability of the group to employ specialization in pursuit of the group goal.[5]

[1] See ch. iii, p. 31, ft. nt. 7.

[2] See ch. ix, p. 191, ft. nt. 4.

[3] For example, "brainstorming," or the Harwold Group Thinkometer, allows each participant to press a button for "yes," "no," or "maybe," thus not endangering his position in the organization with open discussion.

[4] See Lyman Bryson: "Notes on a Theory of Advice," *Polit. Sci. Q.*, Vol. LXVI (1951), pp. 321-9. On the problem-solving superiority of groups low in self-oriented need, see N. T. Fouriezos, M. L. Hutt, and H. Guetzkow: "Measurement of Self-Oriented Needs in Discussion Groups," *J. Abnorm. and Soc. Psychol.*, Vol. XLV (1950), pp. 682-90.

[5] *Resolving Social Conflicts* (New York: Harper & Brothers; 1948).

An organizational decision-making group is ostensibly a small problem-solving group, and so all the experimental data concerning the latter are relevant to the former. These data roughly indicate that the problem-solving process goes through three stages:[6] first, orientation, which includes the statement of the problem, definitions, etc.; secondly, evaluation, or the setting up of relevant values and norms; and thirdly, control, including attempts to influence decision or solution. It is necessary to get agreement at each phase before a joint decision at the control end can be achieved. One of the prerogatives of the superior position in hierarchically structured groups is to monopolize the orientation phase and to define the problem. "We are meeting here for the following purpose." If the problem is thus hierarchically defined, the resulting decision cannot be called a group decision. Although in specific cases particular superiors may forego the exercise of this right, common experience indicates that the right is frequently claimed. Such a hierarchical statement of the problem will almost certainly have inarticulate premises relating to personal goals or to informal group goals, and this fact contributes to the difficulty of obtaining an effective solution.

In a nonstratified group, positive and negative responses of other members act as controls over participants in the direction not only of goal accomplishment but also of eventual consensus, or true group decision. In the stratified, or hierarchical group, high status or prestige protects a person from group influence but increases the power of his own positive or negative reaction as a control over others in the group. The group must yield to him.

It has been observed in experimental groups that the perception of leadership (Who is the leader?) is related to the quantity rather than the quality of his activity.[7] Fur-

[6] See Robert F. Bales: "The Equilibrium Problem in Small Groups," in Talcott Parsons, Robert F. Bales, and Edward A. Shils: *Working Papers in The Theory of Action* (Glencoe, Illinois: The Free Press; 1953), pp. 111-63.

[7] Ibid.

thermore, as groups increase in size, a larger and larger proportion of the activity is addressed to the perceived leader, and he addresses himself more and more to the group as a whole. The process tends to become one of informal lecture with questions and answers, with the familiar rimless wagon wheel or star pattern of communication. In the formal organizational group, the position of "leader" is predefined: he is the person with the highest hierarchical position.[8] Even apart from the *rights* of his position, therefore, there is a strong tendency for him to dominate the group process.

In a group with considerable cohesion, "questions provide a means of turning the process into the instrumental-adaptive direction of movement, with a low probability of provoking an affective reaction; and they are an extremely effective way of turning the initiative over to the other."[9] Questions, however, prevent the asker from improving his status, because the initiative is given over to another. Questions are much less likely, therefore, to be used in a competitive, stratified group.

In the experimental group without formal structure, the idea man is most disruptive of group equilibrium and therefore most likely to arouse hostility. He is also most likely to be perceived as the group leader. In the formally structured group, the idea man is doubly dangerous. He endangers the established distribution of power and status; and he is a competitive threat to his peers. Consequently, he tends to be suppressed.[1]

These potential weaknesses in the group-thinking process in formally structured groups raise the question of how modern organizations manage to make effective decisions.

[8] See W. H. Crockett, "Emergent Leadership in Small, Decision-Making Groups," *J. of Abnorm. Psychol.*, Vol. LI (1955), pp. 378-83.

[9] Bales: loc. cit., p. 127.

[1] Note the growing antipathy to idea men, to brilliance, that pervades our bureaucracies. The average person who will *get along* with others and *go along* with the system is preferred. See Whyte: op. cit., pp. 143 ff.

Four possible answers suggest themselves, each of which is no doubt true to some extent. First, the problems taken up for formal group decision may not usually have a high degree of importance to the organization's success, and a *de facto* delegation of important decisions to informal specialist groups actually takes place.[2] Secondly, it is likely that a considerable degree of self-restraint in the exercise of hierarchical decisional rights must be and usually is practiced.[3] Thirdly, it is possible that formal bureaucratic decisions are not as effective as they could be.[4] And, fourthly, a point to be more fully explored in a later chapter, it is our contention that much of the effective decisional process in organization is camouflaged by myths and fictions to give it an apparent consistency with the culturally sanctioned rights of hierarchy.

4. *Achieving Personal Goals*

As Durkheim said, specialization as an adjustment to achieve a more satisfactory life means performing not only a function which reduces competition but also one suited to a person's constitution or tastes.[5] The organization must be capable, therefore, of satisfying personal goals. It is not only a distribution of powers, capacities, and rights designed to pro-

[2] Does not everyone groan about the uselessness and triviality of all the formal meetings he has to attend? Note that the constant consultation between specialists is actually an informal group-decision process. Often the formal meeting only registers or ritualizes the results of these informal processes. On the subject matter of high-level decisions in business, see Gordon: op. cit., chs. iv, v.

[3] See Chester Barnard: *The Functions of the Executive* (Cambridge: Harvard University Press; 1938), pp. 193-4. He says the "fine art" of executive decisional ability is knowing when *not* to decide.

[4] Note March and Simon's contention that satisficing rather than maximizing norms are usually applied to organization decisions, and that the approval of proposals is as much a function of their source and timing as of their utility. Op. cit., pp. 140-1, 188.

[5] Emile Durkheim: *The Division of Labor in Society*, trans. George Simpson (New York: The Macmillan Co.; 1933), pp. 374-5.

mote an official system of values, but also a means of achieving personal goals.[6]

The ability of an organization to satisfy the personal needs and motives of all its participants is compromised by the definitions of hierarchical roles. In our previous discussion, following March and Simon, we saw that job satisfaction depends upon the degree of skill involved, the variety of activities, the degree of autonomy, the consistency of the job with the individual's self-image, and the predictability of work relationships. These elements of job satisfaction may come into conflict with the superior's right to assign activities and to supervise them. The right of arbitrary command may conflict with cultural norms of independence; and the right to unusual deference may conflict with norms of equality and dignity. The self-images of subordinates are endangered.[7]

Within the hierarchy, the opportunities for job satisfactions other than the exercise of authority are particularly scarce; and this is increasingly so as one mounts the hierarchy, since the specialist element in such jobs becomes increasingly attenuated. Consequently, hierarchical positions are generally oriented to goals such as power, money, and prestige. With the decline in specialist content in hierarchical position there is a corresponding decline in the possibility

[6] On this point see especially the works of Chris Argyris, for example, "The Individual and Organization: Some Problems of Mutual Adjustment," *Admin. Sci. Q.*, Vol. II (1957), pp. 1-22, and "Understanding Human Behavior in Organizations: One Viewpoint," in Mason Haire, ed.: *Modern Organization Theory* (New York: John Wiley & Sons, Inc.; 1959), pp. 115-54. The Argyris approach has been called the "fusion process." It is usefully summarized in John M. Pfiffner and Frank P. Sherwood: *Administrative Organization* (Englewood Cliffs, New Jersey: Prentice-Hall, Inc.; 1960), ch. xx. See also Thomas G. Spates: *Human Values Where People Work* (New York: Harper & Brothers; 1960).

[7] Expectations of independence, equality, and dignity, being cultural, will vary from country to country. Their impact upon organization will, hence, also vary. See Stephen A. Richardson: "Organizational Contrasts on British and American Ships," *Admin. Sci. Q.* (September 1956).

of operational performance standards. Since the distribution
of the more formal and obviously personal rewards of
power, money, and prestige is the prerogative of a superior,
the satisfaction of such personal goals requires conformity
to the superior's demands, whatever they may be. Thus
"brown-nosing," hypocrisy, and "false personalization" [8] are
endemic in modern bureaucracies. This is especially true in
the upper reaches of the hierarchy.[9] Anxiety generated by
nonoperational demands of superiors and by the actual dependence upon subordinates often expresses itself in a preference for bureaupathic practices, such as excessive formal-
ism and impersonality, overstrict compliance with rules and
regulations, and close supervision.[1] The relationship between
hierarchical insecurity and such practices will be discussed
in a later chapter.

The full exercise of hierarchical rights results in autocratic rule, or bureaupathic supervision. Whereas a person
in a hierarchical position can be expected to dislike the insecurity of his own position and the application of autocratic practices to himself, he may be less sensitive to the
reaction of his subordinates to his application of such practices to them. He may even need to impose autocratic
discipline as an outlet for aggressions necessarily repressed

[8] The term is from *The Lonely Crowd,* by David Riesman,
Nathan Glazer, and Reuel Denney (Garden City, New York: Doubleday & Company, Inc.; 1953), see pp. 303-5. See also Harold J. Leavitt:
Managerial Psychology (Chicago: University of Chicago Press; 1958),
p. 264; Moore: op. cit., pp. 142-5.

[9] Also, a kind of natural selection brings to these positions people
who are most strongly motivated by the desire for power, money, and
prestige, the very personal goals most thoroughly under the control of
one's superior.

[1] Anxiety has been defined as a vague, nonspecific fear resulting
from threats to values basic to the integrity of the personality. Rollo
May: *The Meaning of Anxiety* (New York: The Ronald Press Company; 1950), p. 191. The basic values in our society are those related
to social prestige or status, which, in turn, is largely a function of
hierarchical position. Consequently, acute anxiety is a normal condition
within the bureaucratic hierarchy.

in his own role as subordinate.[2] Many studies testify to the deleterious effect of autocratic supervision on the personal satisfactions and goals of subordinates.[3]

The superior's right to monopolize official communication also can be damaging to personal satisfactions or goals. As Lewin has pointed out, denial of pertinent information to participants prevents a cognitive structuring of events and results in emotionalism, lack of direction, alienation, and conflict.[4] When the subordinate is denied information, he is prevented from seeing the relationship between his immediate activities and the larger group objectives, and therefore does not have the satisfaction of knowing he is part of a larger, important, co-operative effort. Although the hierarchical role does not *require* the withholding of information, it does *condone* a certain insensitivity to subordinate needs. Furthermore, strategic considerations surrounding hierarchical competition and the need to protect the legitimacy of roles make for caution in the distribution of information, both to subordinates and to others.[5]

We pointed out above that the currently prevalent concept of organization, the monistic concept, was essentially a verbal formulation of the institution of hierarchy. The monistic concept gives rise to practices and to relationships that duplicate childhood to a considerable extent. In monistic theory at least, although somewhat less in actual practice, each individual in the organization except the top man is subordinate to a parentlike figure who instructs, reviews, admonishes, reproves, praises, criticizes, evaluates, supports, rewards, and punishes, thereby duplicating much of the ex-

[2] See Erich Fromm: *Escape From Freedom* (New York: Holt, Rinehart and Winston, Inc.; 1941).

[3] This statement applies to a society where expectations of democratic treatment predominate. Where people have been brought up to expect autocratic supervision, it would probably not apply. See Cecil A. Gibb: "Leadership," in Gardner Lindzey, ed.: op. cit., pp. 910-12.

[4] Lewin: op. cit.

[5] See ch. viii below. Leavitt says that equalitarian, multichannel communication nets are best but are seldom used because they conflict with hierarchical prerogatives. Op. cit., p. 204.

perience of childhood. This denial of adulthood is surely one of the more painful aspects of modern organization.[6] Furthermore, we suspect that performing the role of the parentlike figure would be equally painful for mature, sensitive adults.

The most serious impact of the hierarchical system upon the achievement of personal goals within organizations results from its appropriation of the definition of success in our culture. Since the time of the Reformation, success in Western civilization has been interpreted in competitive and individualistic terms of relative social prestige or status.[7] Wealth has long been a dominant symbol of status. As we have shown above, status or social prestige, with all of its symbols, including income, has become largely a monopoly of the hierarchy in modern bureaucracy. Bureaucratic hierarchy has inherited the rights and privileges of the early charismatic leader and his retainers, the traditionalistic king and his nobility, and the entrepreneurial owner-manager and his familial protégés. Consequently, to be socially defined as "successful" in our culture, one must proceed up some hierarchy. To have public recognition and esteem,[8] hence self-esteem, one must succeed hierarchically. This situation is painful for the specialist. Even if he is the kind of person

[6] See Leavitt: op. cit., pp. 264-5; and Chris Argyris: op. cit. See also ch. ix, below, and references there cited on p. 182, ft. nt. 5.

[7] See Rollo May: op. cit., pp. 215 ff.; also Abram Kardiner: *The Psychological Frontiers of Society* (New York: Columbia University Press; 1945). Since the dominant symbol of status has been money, "success" in America is usually equated with "making money." See Irvin Gordon Wyllie: *The Self-Made Man in America* (New Brunswick: Rutgers University Press; 1954); Kenneth S. Lynn: *The Dream of Success* (Boston: Little, Brown & Co.; 1955); Richard D. Mosier: *Making the American Mind* (New York: King's Crown Press; 1947).

[8] Some social scientists use "esteem" to refer to the evaluation of role enactment, and "prestige" to refer to the deference ranking of the position. However, the confusion of person and position involved in the hierarchical status system is likewise a confusion of prestige and esteem. By virtue of one's hierarchical position he acquires prestige, hence income, hence social esteem. Nonhierarchical positions, such as medical doctor, give a person the prestige attached to the position, but he must earn his esteem by good role performance.

who can satisfy his dominance needs by mastering a skill
rather than people, he will be denied "success" unless he
gives up his specialty and enters hierarchical competition.[9]
A corollary of the hierarchical appropriation of success is
the derogation of intellect, imagination, and skill so prevalent in modern bureaucracy.[1]

As we pointed out above, the status system apportions
according to hierarchical position important personal satisfactions such as power, income, deference, interesting opportunities and associations. This tendency is reinforced by
the fact that persons in hierarchical positions have greater
opportunities to manipulate the organization in the interest
of their own personal goals.[2] These opportunities result
from the superior's strategic power to satisfy or to frustrate
the personal goals of others in the organizational unit; from
his ability to control the flow of official communication;
from his hierarchical rights toward subordinates—for example,
the institutionalized plagiarism involved in the obligation to
use the boss's signature; and from the fact that superiors
cannot practically be subjected to very close supervision by
their superiors. The resulting maldistribution causes a sense
of injustice within organizations and a suspicion of the upper hierarchy, the "management." [3] This general sense of

[9] Moore: op. cit., ch. vi; Alvin W. Gouldner: *Patterns of Industrial Bureaucracy* (Glencoe, Illinois: The Free Press; 1954), p. 226; and
Riesman, *et al.*: op. cit., pp. 154-5, all report this fact.

[1] See Whyte: op. cit., ch. x, and *passim*.

[2] See Philip Selznick: "An Approach to a Theory of Bureaucracy, *Am. Sociol. Rev.*, Vol. VIII (1943). The office, because of its
advantages, comes to be regarded as an end rather than a means. For
this process in labor unions, see A. J. Muste: "Factional Fights in Trade
Unions," in J. B. S. Hardman, ed.: *American Labor Dynamics* (New
York: Harcourt, Brace & Co.; 1928).

[3] Many people report this general sense of injustice resulting from
the hierarchically skewed distribution system. See, for example, Barnard: "The Functions and Pathology of Status Systems in Formal
Organizations," op. cit.; Moore: op. cit., p. 184; Fritz Roethlisberger:
Management and Morale (Cambridge: Harvard University Press; 1941),
p. 77; Peter Drucker: *The New Society: The Anatomy of the Industrial Order* (New York: Harper & Brothers; 1950), pp. 92-5.

injustice reduces the willingness and the ability to co-operate, thereby sabotaging the promise of specialization.

This damage to co-operativeness is increased by the hierarchical appropriation of success. Employees of our modern organizations are culturally conditioned to expect promotions for good work. With some exceptions in professional specializations, as for instance junior chemist to chemist to senior chemist, promotions are defined as improvement in hierarchical rank. But the number of hierarchical positions decreases rapidly, and so opportunities for promotions, so defined, are extremely limited. Furthermore, above a very low level of actual operations, "merit" becomes an essentially subjective judgment of superiors, despite the attempted quantification with formal performance-rating schemes.[4] Furthermore, above very low hierarchical levels, the admission of new persons into the hierarchy is best described as sponsorship and co-optation. The crucial questions are not merit and ability in the ordinary sense, but the compatibility and loyalty of the newcomers from the standpoint of the existing management "team." "Is he our kind?"[5] The result of these various considerations is that many persons of great merit according to one set of criteria will nevertheless be "failures" in our society. Since they have been led to expect promotion for good work, they will interpret their nonpromotion as rejection by superiors and the organization as a whole. As March and Simon point out, this feeling of rejection is

[4] See Norman J. Powell: *Personnel Administration in Government* (Englewood Cliffs, New Jersey: Prentice-Hall, Inc.; 1956), chs. xi, xvi; Moore: op. cit., p. 143; and Leavitt: op. cit., pp. 259-62.

[5] See ch. vii below; also C. Wright Mills: *The Power Elite* (New York: Oxford University Press, Inc.; 1957), ch. vi. Since the operationality of performance standards declines as we go up the hierarchy (see Moore: op. cit., pp. 140-3, and March and Simon: op. cit., p. 63), the superior's rights with relation to the subordinate's ambitions or personal needs become more and more analogous to political power; the process of climbing the hierarchy or "getting ahead" becomes more and more a political process; and the kind of person who can succeed at this game becomes more and more like the political type. On this point generally, see Harold Lasswell: *Politics: Who Gets What, When, How* (New York: McGraw-Hill Book Co.; 1936).

less painful if the persons involved do not identify with the organization.[6] The definitions and structures of modern bureaucratic organizations are therefore not compatible with a high degree of organizational identification, and one basis of co-operation, that of group cohesion, is lost.

The hierarchical role system, with its associated privileges and prerogatives, its power over personal goals, and its near monopoly of "success," results in considerable denial of social recognition and status for large numbers of people in modern organizations. The resulting dissatisfactions are no basis for the kind of solidarity which could make increasing specialization work easily.[7]

The foregoing discussion of the relationships between specialist and hierarchical roles in the accomplishment of organizational and personal goals provides a basis for the analysis of conflict in modern organizations. Concerning conflict in industrial bureaucracy, Melville Dalton has said: "Approached sociologically, relations among members of management in the plants could be viewed as a general conflict system caused and perpetuated chiefly by (1) power struggles . . . from competition between departments . . . ; (2) drives . . . to increase . . . status; (3) conflict between union and management; and (4) the staff-line friction. . . ."[8] Without in any way disagreeing with Dalton, we view the pattern of intraorganizational conflict as arising from the inter-

[6] March and Simon: op. cit., p. 74. See also R. C. Stone: "Mobility Factors as they Affect Workers' Attitudes and Conduct toward Incentive Systems," *Am. Sociol. Rev.*, Vol. XVII (1952), pp. 58-64.

[7] On the possible kinds of adaptations to this sort of frustrated ambition, see Robert K. Merton: "Social Structure and Anomie," in *Social Theory and Social Structure* (Glencoe, Illinois: The Free Press; 1957), pp. 131 ff. See also, Moore: op. cit., pp. 267-70; Charles A. Drake: "When Wage Incentives Fail," *Advanced Management*, Vol. VII (1942), pp. 42-4; and Whiting Williams: *Main-Springs of Men* (New York: Charles Scribner's Sons; 1925).

[8] "Conflicts between Line and Staff Managerial Officers," *Am. Sociol. Rev.*, Vol. XV (1950), pp. 342-51. He points out that the intensity of the conflict was exaggerated because recognition of the conflict had to be repressed.

In the following discussion we do not wish to leave the impression that we believe conflict per se is bad.

actions between the principal behavior systems in these organizations: the system of rights, or authority; the system of deference, or status; the system of specialization, or the distribution of abilities, which governs the pattern of technical interdependence; and the system of communicative interaction which governs the pattern of identifications. We shall discuss conflict under three general organizing topics: (1) conflict due to the violation of role expectations; (2) conflict concerning the reality of interdependence; and (3) conflict arising from blocks to spontaneous communication.

5. Conflict: Role Expectations

The newer specialties in organizations are usually lumped together conceptually under the name "staff specialties." A number of upsetting relationships arise from these new specialties. In the first place, they threaten older specialties with the loss of functions or with the addition of new unwanted ones. Especially is this so if the centralizations involved in the new specialties result from the exercise of the hierarchical prerogative to assign duties and to create jobs, rather than from the social advance of specialization.[9] Apart from such acts of power, however, the new specialty must achieve social accreditation before it is accepted.

Advancing specialization upsets status expectations as well as vested interests in functions. Specialization, by giving a function to everyone, brings low- and high-status persons into interdependent relationships, thereby violating the status expectations of the latter.[1]

The "staff" threat to function and status is particularly acute with regard to hierarchical, or "line," positions low enough down to contain specialist content.[2] In fact, the con-

[9] Dalton's study showed only 50 per cent of staff people doing work related to their college training, thereby casting doubt on the validity of some of the specializations. Loc. cit.

[1] In Dalton's study, staff specialties were the new ones and these specialists were much younger on the average than others in the organization. "Line" resistance was especially pronounced. Dalton: loc. cit.

[2] Dalton: loc. cit.; Moore: op. cit., ch. vi.

flict arising from these new specialties is usually designated as the line-staff conflict. Since specialties eventually win legitimacy one way or another, they acquire authority of a nonhierarchical kind which invades the domain of hierarchical authority. In this way there arises a growing discrepancy between *expected authority* and *actual authority* which lies at the heart of the line-staff conflict. Mechanisms of hierarchical protection against this threat of specialization will be discussed in later chapters. Here we wish only to call attention to the universally adopted devices of derogating staff importance ("Line is more important than staff.") and of attempting to suppress recognition of the unpalatable features of the relationship by the use of fictions ("Staff only advises; it does not command.").

6. Conflict: Reality of Interdependence

Much conflict in organization concerns the *reality* of interdependence. As we pointed out above, part of this conflict is due to differing perceptions of reality between persons in specialist and hierarchical positions. The need for the new specialty, hence the new interdependence, may also be questioned by existing specialists because of fear of loss of function. More important from the standpoint of conflict in organizations is disagreement as to the need for new interdependence which arises when rights or competencies are allocated by the hierarchy in disregard of technical needs. As we pointed out above, one of the rights of hierarchical positions is the right to delegate rights or authority. It is possible for rights, for example the right to review or to be consulted, to be distributed in a manner inconsistent with the distribution of ability. It is possible for competencies to be defined in defiance of the needs of specialization.

The existence of such authority to ignore the needs of specialization, this possibility of pure acts of political power, opens the way for interpersonal and intergroup competition for authority and jurisdiction. An ambitious person may bring more activities and more people under his jurisdiction, thereby increasing his power and status, by two methods. He may contrive to get himself promoted to a higher hierarchical position; or he may get rights reallocated so as to increase his jurisdiction. The first method, being more legitimate, is less likely to arouse conflict; but, as we have seen, promotional opportunities are inherently scarce in relation to demand and may not in any case be available to a particular person because of the sponsorship system prevailing in the organization. The second method, therefore, that of expanding jurisdiction, may be the only one practically available. Furthermore, if a given group of subordinates seeks status vicariously through identification with its superior and with its organizational unit, its influence will be directed toward an expansion of jurisdiction. Also, as pointed out above, since the hierarchy is more impressed by the need for joint decision than are others in the organization, its defenses against attempts to expand jurisdiction are weakened, resulting in much unnecessary interdependence in bureaucracy. Since expansion of one jurisdiction often means the diminution of another, this method of increasing status produces conflict.

It is likely that newer specialties are more expansionist than old ones, deprived as they are of the full measure of their expected status and function because of lack of full acceptance.[3] If the new specialty is a hierarchical creation rather than a result of the advance of specialization, expansionism probably reflects an attempt to allay the inevitable insecurity associated with an imbalance between authority and ability, that is to say, the *right* to be consulted is greater than the *ability* to make a contribution.[4] However,

[3] Dalton says that staff people have less chance of hierarchical advance and hence must engage in empire-building activities. Dalton: loc. cit.

[4] The concept of the imbalance between authority and ability is essentially the same as the concept of the imbalance between authority and power in political and historical analysis. For example, the *authority* of the French nobility fell before the *power* of the French middle class, meaning the latter's growing monopoly of relevant abilities—abilities to provision the nation, to keep essential services coming. On

expansionism may also reflect simply the attempt by a newer specialty to realize a full measure of function consistent with its technical promise. In this latter case, free interaction between the new and the old will eventually cure the cause of conflict, allowing the new to demonstrate its validity and hence the need for the new interdependence.[5] But conflict arising from resistance to new interdependence arbitrarily imposed can be eliminated only by redefining jurisdictions to accord with the real technical needs of the situation, or by a defeatist acceptance of the new jurisdictions. In the latter case, any change in the distribution of political power in the organization, power which comes from the personal support of persons with power, will likely be followed by more or less intense activity seeking to reallocate rights of jurisdiction. In this way, an allocation of rights by arbitrary authority creates an unstable and potentially explosive situation.

A common form of conflict concerning interdependence is that which sometimes arises over the joint use of means. When centralization is undertaken to allow full employment of the latest specializations in skills or equipment, the minor conflicts from joint use which arise because of some inevitable degree of scarcity are not important and are easily resolved without destroying co-operation. The amount of denial and frustration involved can be shown to be necessary and thus acceptable. When the centralization of means is an act of power, however, frustrations arising from the interdependence cannot be made acceptable because they cannot be demonstrated to be necessary. Attempts to ameliorate the

---

this point, see Samuel H. Beer and Adam B. Ulam, eds.: *Patterns of Government* (New York: Random House; 1958), Part One.

[5] It should be noted that specialist organizations may block this free interaction and thus slow up the integration of the new with the old and the adjustment of the old to the new for considerable periods of time. The activities of building trades-unions are notorious examples of this process, but the same elements are at work, for example, in medical resistance to a redefinition of nurses' roles. See Harvey L. Smith: "Contingencies of Professional Differentiation," *Am. J. Sociol.*, Vol. LXIII (1958), pp. 410-14.

conflict by the permanent, full-time assignment of subunits of means to each client cannot remove the instability in the situation, disclosing as it does the fact that the centralization in question is purely a matter of right, of authority, with none of the requirements of specialization involved. Whenever it is technically possible permanently to assign subunits of means, it is technically possible to decentralize.

To illustrate our point, suppose Miss Brown is the subordinate of Mr. Jones and that she is his stenographer. The organization then decides to centralize stenography by creating a stenographic pool. Miss Brown is transferred to the pool but, to avoid conflict over the joint use of means, she is permanently assigned to Mr. Jones. Her technical relationship to Mr. Jones is the same; she is his stenographer. However, authority relationships have been changed. She is now the subordinate of Mrs. Smith, the pool chief, rather than of Mr. Jones. The centralization was an act of pure authority. Only authority relationships were involved.

We should point out that part of the difficulties which arise from centralization can be traced back to the monocratic character of the hierarchical institution. We have said that activities are frequently centralized to assure full employment of the latest specialization in skills or equipment by concentrating demand for them. However, if the new specialist could be a member of several organizational units instead of one, this centralization of activities would not be necessary. It is held that such multiple membership would violate the principle of "unity of command" and must therefore be avoided. The reason it is avoided, however, is that it is incompatible with the institution of hierarchy. It would place the specialist in the subordinate relationship with more than one superior; he would have more than one *boss* and the rights of the superordinate role preclude more than one boss. The hierarchical institution is monocratic. Among the many suggestions which Frederick Taylor made, his suggestion for several "functional foremen" for each operator was never taken seriously by management. Such an arrangement would attack the very heart of the institution of hierarchy.

7. Conflict: Communication Patterns

We have discussed role conflicts and conflicts concerning the reality of interdependence, or the need for joint decision. There is also conflict over goals. To the extent that goal conflict is organizationally determined, it arises from the communication patterns in the organization. A great deal of interpersonal communication works toward a common conception of reality and the sharing of goals. Conversely, barriers to such communication result in differentiation of reality perception and of goals.[6] The communication pattern in an organization, therefore, results in groups—clusters of people who, by virtue of frequent and free interaction, within the limits of their own particular group share goals and reality perceptions.

The pattern of interaction is determined by the principal behavior systems in organizations. Involved are the systems of authority, status, and specialization, the system of technically necessary interdependence in regard to the organization's goal. The pyramidal distribution of hierarchical rights tends strongly to create groups composed of subordinates and a superior in a wagon wheel pattern of communication.[7] The hierarchical control of official communication

[6] See March and Simon: op. cit., pp. 124-9. They distinguish between *cognitive* and *affective* elements in goal sharing and goal differentiation. Both, however, are mediated through communication. Although this distinction can be made analytically, it may not be of too much practical importance because both elements would seem to be inextricably combined. My *knowledge* of my goal performs a psychological function and is therefore valued, is *affectively* backed up. Group goals help maintain the cohesiveness of the group and are therefore valued for similar reasons.

[7] Under strictly autocratic practices, the pattern of communication would be star-shaped; little group identification would result. As the group composed of supervisor and subordinates becomes more cohesive, the structure of the communication pattern changes until it is difficult to tell who is the formal head, and in fact most communication may eventually be directed to a person other than the appointed head—to an "informal leader." When this development occurs, the

tends to divide the organization into management (hierarchy) and employees (labor). The status system, with its blocks to interaction between strata, reinforces this division and both together alienate the group, the "employees," from the organization as a whole. Shared goals and reality perceptions do not easily extend across this barrier.

Hierarchical control of official communication in conjunction with the status system subdivides the whole organization into status strata. Although there are status strata among purely specialist positions, as for example, junior classification analyst, analyst, and senior analyst, and general status divisions between clerical and professional and blue collar and white collar, the heavily emphasized status divisions correspond to hierarchical rank. Status blocks to interaction between strata prevent the development of common goals and perceptions of reality, creating some degree of alienation from the organization, stratum by stratum, diminishing as one goes up the ladder of strata.

This alienation within the hierarchy is reduced by two factors. First, mobile individuals, expecting to climb to high positions, try to adopt or to appear to adopt the values and reality perceptions of higher levels.[8] Secondly, through the practice of sponsorship, certain likely individuals at lower levels are chosen early and "groomed" for high-management positions.[9] By virtue of these various forces and mech-

---

formal head has accepted the obligations of group membership and has rejected his hierarchical duties and forfeited his hierarchical rights.

[8] See Merton: "Continuities in the Theory of Reference Groups and Social Structure," op. cit., ch. ix.

[9] See Mills: op. cit., ch. vi; Everett C. Hughes: "Queries Concerning Industry and Society Growing Out of Study of Ethnic Relations in Industry," *Am. Sociol. Rev.*, Vol. XIV (1949), pp. 218-20; Orvis Collins: "Ethnic Behavior in Industry: Sponsorship and Rejection in a New England Factory," *Am. J. of Sociol.*, Vol. LI (1946), pp. 293-8; Joseph W. Eaton: "Is Scientific Leadership Selection Possible?," *Am. J. of Sociol.* (1947); E. L. Thorndike: *Human Nature and the Social Order* (New York: The Macmillan Co.; 1940); W. Kornhauser: "The Negro Union Official: A Study of Sponsorship and Control," *Am. J. of Sociol.*, Vol. LVII (1952), pp. 443-52; Melville Dalton: "Informal Factors in Career Achievements," *Am. J. of Sociol.*, Vol. LVI (1951).

anisms, the "management group" is actually much smaller than the total number of those in supervisory positions; and, in fact, it is customary these days to speak of a still smaller "inner cabinet" or "top management" composed of the head of the organization and his immediate subordinates.

The system of specialization requires the interaction of persons whose specialties must be harmonized in order to achieve the organizational goal. This interaction is restricted both by the distribution of authority, hierarchical and delegated, and by the groupings formed by the official communication system. The superior's right to be the sole source of influence over subordinates, or the "unity of command"; his right fully to be apprised of what is going on, or his right of supervision; his right to monopolize communication; his right to the loyalty of his subordinates—all restrict free interaction between subordinate specialists of one organizational unit and those of another. Reinforcing these restrictions are the demands of the individual's immediate work group, including fellow subordinates and possibly his superior, that he share and give effect to their values and perceptions of reality. Although his status grouping may also interfere with communication with a lower-level specialist, it is our belief that this factor is not serious in purely specialist interaction.[1]

Despite these restrictions, interaction is technically necessary; and since no formal unit, work group, or status stratum could contain all the relevant specialties, specialist interaction must take place across formal unit and status-stratum lines. As we have mentioned above, this necessary interaction carves out specialist channels of communication, and therefore channels of influence, of a semi-illegal nature. More important, it leads to the sharing of values and reality

[1] We are arguing, for example, that a senior economist will have little difficulty dealing with a junior statistician in another unit who can actually perform some service that the economist requires. For the chief of the economic section to deal with the same junior statistician would be more painful. On the strains between scientists and the hierarchy in industrial laboratories, see: Simon Marcson: *The Scientist in American Industry* (New York: Harper & Brothers; 1960).

perceptions between the specialists, or to multiple group membership, and also, perhaps, to divided loyalties, doubts, and feelings of guilt. Interunit conflict becomes internalized in the individual. All of these effects are likely to be reinforced by the specialist's dependence upon specialist lines and channels for personal satisfactions of status and function, unless he is willing to forego his specialty and enter hierarchical competition. Finally, we should point out that the dimensions of the dilemma of specialist interaction are qualified by the importance of the interdependence, by whether the interdependence involves functional necessities or only working conveniences, for example, the clearance of proposed new programs or the installation of an additional telephone extension.[2]

The bases of intraorganizational conflict can be summarized in a few general propositions, as follows:[3]

    1. Conflict is a function of disagreement over the reality of interdependence.

        1.1. Lack of agreement about the reality of interdependence arises from lack of acceptance of specialties.

        This lack of acceptance results from lack of accreditation of specialties, which, in turn, is a function of

        1.1.1. Their newness, or

        1.1.2. The creation of specialties by acts of authority.

        1.2. Lack of agreement about the reality of interdependence is also a function of differing perceptions of reality. These differing perceptions are a function of position in

        1.2.1. The authority system,

[2] It should be noted, however, that trivia may have great symbolical significance. Much of the conflict in organizations has a trivial origin.

[3] We should emphasize again that we are discussing *only* organizationally generated phenomena. Conflict also results from extraorganizational influences such as the general social conditioning that shapes personality, conflicting group affiliations, racial and religious attitudes, etc.

1.2.2. The status system, and

1.2.3. The system of person-to-person communication (the group system).

2. Conflict is a function of the degree of disparity between authority, the right to be consulted, and the ability to contribute to goals. This disparity arises from

2.1. Growing dependence upon specialists (a function of the process of specialization) while hierarchical role definitions are changing more slowly; and

2.2. The allocation of rights (delegation) in disregard of the needs of specialization (acts of sheer authority).

3. Conflict is a function of the degree of status violation involved in interaction.

3.1. Status violation results from advancing specialization and consequent growing interdependence of high- and low-status positions—from positional claims to deference, on the one hand, and the fact of dependence upon specialists, on the other.

4. Conflict is made more or less intense by the relative importance of the interdependence to the success of the organization.

5. Finally, conflict is a function of the lack of shared values and reality perceptions (identifications), which, in addition to being a function of personalities, are

5.1. A function of the lack of spontaneity and freedom of communicative interaction, which is

5.1.1. A function of the resistance to penetration from without of the principal behavior systems—the authority system, the status system, and the technical system (specialization).

In short, conflict arises from growing inconsistencies between specialist and hierarchical roles. Whereas there are other bases for conflict, it is likely that they could easily be managed under a regime of specialist solidarity based upon the mutual recognition of the need for interdependence. The resolution of these conflicts in modern organization is made difficult by virtue of the fact that they are not formally recognized or legitimated. To legitimate them would be inconsistent with the monocratic nature of hierarchy. It would require formal bargaining procedures.[4] Modern organizations, through the formal hierarchy of authority, seek an "administered consensus."[5] The resolution of these conflicts, therefore, must occur informally by surreptitious and somewhat illegal means.

8. *Role Protection*

The conflict between specialist and hierarchical roles has generated mechanisms of role defense. From the standpoint of the hierarchical role, defense involves the securing and maintenance of the legitimacy of the role. The legitimation of hierarchical roles will be discussed in the next several chapters. Here we wish only to set forth some of the mechanisms of specialist role defense.

We have already mentioned that in order to claim "success" as culturally defined, the specialist must give up his specialty and enter hierarchical competition. A person who chooses this course of action must adopt the values of the managerial group to which he aspires. This "anticipatory socialization" enables such a person to avoid the worst consequences of specialist-hierarchical conflict.[6] Merton has pointed out that a specialist not wishing to follow this path may adopt a sort of schizoid separation of his roles, maintaining his own values privately and relating himself to the organization solely in his specialist or technical capacity. Accordingly, he refuses to take any responsibility for the use or nonspecialist consequences of his advice, regarding such

4 See ch. vi.
5 The term was suggested to me by Robert Presthus. Also see p. 99, ft. nt. 8.
6 See Merton: op. cit., pp. 265-71. Conscious, opportunistic adoption of managerial values is likely to involve the specialist in difficulties with his peers who will regard him as "pushy," a "climber," a person "bucking for a promotion," an "upstart," and even a "renegade."

matters as "policy questions" to be handled by the "administrative people." Much specialist training, especially of engineers, contains a liberal amount of preparation for such subaltern status.[7]

We have also pointed out that specialists engaged in organizational problem solving consistently evade official prescriptions in order to get the job done, especially in the matter of communication. This evasion of official prescriptions also takes place in the lower levels of the hierarchy where hierarchical positions contain a good deal of specialist content, perhaps mostly specialist content.[8]

An increasingly used device of specialist role protection is the formation of local, state, and national associations of specialists. These associations compensate to some extent for lack of rights of appeal from hierarchical vetos by providing a "free constituency" to which vetoed items may be presented.[9] Although some professional associations may function as devices of managerial control of specialists (perhaps some engineering associations have so functioned in the past), it would seem that most of them severely limit managerial control by specifying just how their members

[7] Merton: op. cit., chs. vii and xvii. Others have pointed out that technical specialists are generally easy for power-seekers to manipulate. See Hans H. Gerth and C. Wright Mills: "A Marx for the Managers," *Ethics*, Vol. LII (1941-2), pp. 200-15. The specialized training acts as a blinder to other aspects of experience. Veblen referred to this phenomenon as "trained incapacity."

[8] See Melville Dalton: "Unofficial Union-Management Relations," *Am. Sociol. Rev.*, Vol. XV (1950), pp. 611-19. This study shows that lower-level management officials and lower-level union officials both evade the prescriptions of their respective hierarchies in order to solve their mutual problems. See also Charles Hunt Page: "Bureaucracy's Other Face," *Social Forces*, Vol. XXV (1946), pp. 88-94.

[9] On this point see Bryson: loc. cit.; Philip Selznick: *TVA and The Grass Roots*, (Berkeley: University of California Press; 1949), especially pp. 145-7; and David Truman: *The Governmental Process* (New York: Alfred A. Knopf; 1951), *passim*. Because ideas in bureaucratic organizations are not considered on their merits alone, it would seem reasonable to argue that these "free constituencies" are a necessary condition of organization success in the long run.

may be employed in organizations.[1] In short, they are devices for protecting specialist status and function.

Where a particular skill is concentrated under one or a few employers, that is, in a specific organization, efforts of the skill group to protect its status and function are more effective, resulting in distinctive career groups and peculiar "problems of personnel administration." Examples of such career groups in government organizations are the United States Forest Service, the Geological Survey, social workers, police, firemen, school teachers, public-health workers. Protective activities of such groups result in strong attachments to the careers and the organizations through which they are pursued, emphasis upon objective or proceduralized distribution of recognition and status, life commitments to the careers, a long-range program for the whole career, etc.[2]

Finally, we should mention that pressures for "due process" proceduralized protection of employees have specialist rather than hierarchical origins. They originate both in the new specialties of personnel administration and in the employee associations, whether the latter be called unions or professional societies.

9. Personality versus Role

In closing this chapter, we wish to emphasize again that we have been discussing role interaction, pure organization theory, and not the interaction of personality systems. Since *persons* perform roles, there is bound to be variation in actual role performances. One superior has authoritarian leanings, while another is deeply humanitarian and democratic.

[1] Note, for example, how the Group for the Advancement of Psychiatry seeks to determine the activities of the various specialists in mental institutions. The role of the social worker is defined in the GAP Report Number 16; the role of the "Consultant Psychiatrist in a Family Service or Welfare Agency," in GAP Letter Number 259; etc.

[2] See Wallace S. Sayre and Frederick C. Mosher: *An Agenda for Research in Public Personnel Administration* (Washington, D.C.: National Planning Association; 1959), pp. 37-42.

One specialist cannot see the nose in front of his face, while another has broad vision beyond his specialty. The interaction of personality and role is an important subject, but it is not the subject of this book. At some point power and personality merge.[3]

Our concern is to develop a structural theory of bureaucratic organizations including the human-behavior structures of which they are composed. Confusion of these two areas of study—personality and role—has resulted in a spate of works dealing with questions like leadership or the "functions of the executive." These functions are found to be generalizations based upon the behavior of particular *persons* observed by particular writers, whereas an organization is a structure made up of positions and roles that people move in and out of without destroying the organization. Many of the leadership studies contain the same confusion of personality and role, manifested in this case by the common identification of leadership with headship. A particular personality configuration will meet the requirements of a specific group situation better than another, and this fact gives rise to a leadership *function*. Leadership is a group *function;* headship is a bundle of rights and duties to a superior —a position and a role, a matter of definition. A more detailed discussion of this confusion of personality and position, a charismatic tendency, and its function with regard to the legitimizing of hierarchical authority is reserved for the next chapter.

[3] See Harold Lasswell: *Power and Personality* (New York: W. W. Norton & Company, Inc.; 1948), especially ch. iii.

CHAPTER 6

Ideology

🏵

1. Role Defense and the Decline of Legitimacy

Fᴿᴏᴹ ᴏᴜʀ ᴅɪsᴄᴜssɪᴏɴ of bureaucracy thus far, it is clear
that many developments are threatening the legitimacy of
hierarchical rights, or, to put it another way, the legitimacy of bureaucratic authority. Whereas the legitimacy of a
system probably depends ultimately on nonrational, charismatic elements of some kind,[1] growth of bureaucracy coincides with the decline of charisma in modern life. The decline of the propensity to be impressed by the charismatic
threatens the legitimacy of hierarchical positions. The growing power of specialization over organizational goal achievement and the widening gap between ability and authority
further endanger the legitimacy of these positions.

Originating as they did in predemocratic times, hierarchical role definitions find themselves increasingly at odds
with democratic norms. The resulting pressures are reinforced by the advance of specialization, seeking ever, as it

[1] See Talcott Parsons: *The Structure of Social Action* (New
York: McGraw-Hill Book Co.; 1937), p. 665.

does, the elimination of inequalities and restraints on individual development.[2] The skewed distribution resulting from hierarchical deference or status results in a sense of injustice which is enhanced by the declining legitimacy of hierarchical roles. This declining legitimacy makes it easier for other members of organizations to adopt the hierarchy as a point of reference for evaluating their own lot. This comparison causes dissatisfaction and criticism and suspicion of the hierarchy. Positions in the corporate business hierarchy have their own special problems of role defense in addition to these. Gone are most of the charismatic owner-manager entrepreneurs of yesterday, and this loss of charismatic leadership threatens the power of businessmen in our society.[3] At the same time that the charismatic image of the businessman is slowly fading, the skewed distribution of organizational values reaches its highest point in the hierarchy of corporate bureaucracy, which has largely replaced the older individual enterprise system as the road to wealth and power.

For people who thoroughly accept our modern organizations, the problem posed by these developments, all results of advancing specialization, is how to protect hierarchical position and role as presently defined, with its many powers

[2] Emile Durkheim: *The Division of Labor in Society*, trans. George Simpson (New York: The Macmillan Co.; 1933).

[3] Witness the rise of labor organization and government regulation. See Alvin W. Gouldner: *Studies in Leadership: Leadership and Democratic Action* (New York: Harper & Brothers; 1950), pp. 133 ff. Sumner Slichter says business power has also been weakened by the loss of dependable white-collar support and divisions of interest within the business community. "The Power Holders in the American Economy," *Sat. Eve. Post* (December 13, 1958), pp. 34 ff. We may also remind the reader that the Great Depression struck a powerful blow at the charisma of the business leader. Whereas popular biographies used to be about businessmen, now they tend to be about celebrities of various kinds. Leo Lowenthal: "Biographies in Popular Magazines," in Paul F. Lazarsfeld and Frank Stanton, eds.: *Radio Research, 1942–43*, pp. 507-48. See also David Riesman, Nathan Glazer, and Reuel Denney: *The Lonely Crowd* (Garden City, New York: Doubleday & Company, Inc.; 1953), pp. 239 ff.

and privileges. It is a problem of shoring up the legitimacy of these role definitions, and consequently the legitimacy of authority in modern bureaucracy. This problem has given rise to three kinds of defensive behavior. First, systems of ideas and beliefs supportive of hierarchical prerogatives have been accepted and developed—the *ideological* approach. Secondly, persons in hierarchical positions seek to control the impressions of others about the nature of these positions and their accompanying roles—the *dramaturgical* approach. Finally, we often notice a rigid and ritualistic performance of roles as an attempted escape from insecurity—the *"bureaupathic"* approach. We do not wish to suggest that hierarchies have consciously and conspiratorially formulated these mechanisms of role defense, but rather that we can deduce the existence of the problem from the prevalence of defensive behaviors. In this chapter we shall discuss the ideological approach to role defense, and in the following two chapters the other two approaches will be discussed.

2. *Role Defense through Ideology*

In social science, the ability to influence another person in a somewhat predictable way is called "power." If this influence is sanctified by beliefs, if it is "legitimate," it is called "authority." To avoid dependence upon brute force, power-holders seek legitimacy as a basis for power. They find and develop ideas which justify their power, and these ideas have been called "ideology." [4] Generally, the justifications seek to show that those holding power are most qualified to do so, or that the present authority system is best for all, or that it is *right* in some other sense. Attention is diverted from the institutional structure, and any apparent evils are alleged to arise from the nature of things or from defects of individuals, never from the structure itself. Critics

[4] Karl Mannheim: *Ideology and Utopia* (New York: Harcourt, Brace & Co.; 1936). See also Philip Selznick: "An Approach to a Theory of Bureaucracy," *Am. Sociol. Rev.*, Vol. VIII (1943).

of institutional structure are misinformed or short-sighted.[5]

This discussion of some of the ideological legitimations of bureaucratic authority is not intended to be a scientific evaluation of the ideas involved. We wish merely to point out some of the ideological implications of these ideas. Regardless of its merits otherwise, any system of thought or ideas may have ideological implications in reference to some institutional structure, and acceptance of the ideas in no way implies a cynical opportunism. If one of the tendencies of the ideas is to preserve a given structure, that tendency is an ideological one, whether or not we may agree that the structure in question should be preserved.

The development of ideas is chiefly an academic specialty, and for the most part the ideologues of bureaucracy have been recruited from academe.[6] As a result of their labors, several ideological approaches have emerged which are important in legitimating bureaucratic authority. We shall discuss three: studies of leadership; sociological investigations of the human relations of the work situation ("managerial sociology");[7] and monistic theory of hierarchical

[5] Selznick: loc. cit.; Robert K. Merton: *Social Theory and Social Structure* (Glencoe, Illinois: The Free Press; 1957), pp. 155-7; Gouldner: op. cit., *passim*.

[6] By locating the seeds of bureaucratic power in a historical law of increasing rationality, Max Weber provided the basis for a managerial countermyth to oppose the class myth of Marx. This countermyth becomes a full-fledged managerial dialectic of history at the hands of James Burnham: *The Managerial Revolution: What Is Happening in the World* (New York: The John Day Co.; 1941). See H. Gerth and C. Wright Mills: "A Marx for the Managers," *Ethics*, Vol. LII (1941-2), pp. 200-15. Whyte makes the point that the businessman is dependent upon the academic for the legitimation of his power. By and large he blames the academic rather than the businessman for the direction in which organization behavior is developing. *The Organization Man* (Garden City, New York: Doubleday & Company, Inc.; 1957), ch. viii, especially pp. 119-20.

[7] See Harold L. Sheppard: "The Treatment of Unionism in 'Managerial Sociology,'" *Am. Sociol. Rev.*, Vol XIV (1940), pp. 310-13. Although Sheppard's suggested term was meant to be critical of his scientific brothers, note a recent text by Harold J. Leavitt entitled *Mana-*

responsibility. The first approach is related to the decline of charisma in modern bureaucracy. The second seeks ways of fitting individuals into the bureaucratic structure. The two are closely related because the adjustment of the individual to the organization is allegedly facilitated by skillful leadership. The third approach is part of the monistic conception of hierarchical roles.

3. Leadership

We shall discuss the leadership studies first. Alvin Gouldner suggests that the increasing interest in leadership in this country results from the declining prestige of the businessman, now a bureaucrat, and from the growing alienation of the masses.[8] From the beginning these studies have conceived leadership in charismatic terms, characterizing the leader as a great person who is born to lead.[9] Traits of leadership were consequently sought, and heroic traits were allegedly "found," such as self-control, assiduity, common sense, judgment, justice, enthusiasm, perseverence, tact, courage, faith, loyalty, etc.[1] Although social psychologists have generally concluded by now that there are no leadership traits, that leadership is a function of the situation, including the kind of people, the kind of problem, the kind of group, etc., such studies are continued by business schools and individuals who seek the traits of successful executives.[2]

gerial Psychology (Chicago: University of Chicago Press; 1958). In spite of the title, we think this book is a very good one.

[8] Gouldner: op. cit., pp. 10-11.

[9] Daniel Bell says most of the literature stems from Aristotle and Machiavelli, and contains the two aristocratic images of the mindless masses and the strong-willed leader. "Notes on Authoritarian and Democratic Leadership," in Gouldner: op. cit.

[1] Taken from Arthur Harrison Miller: Leadership (New York: G. P. Putnam's Sons; 1920). See also Edward L. Munson: The Management of Men (New York: Henry Holt and Co.; 1921), and Emory S. Bogardus: Fundamentals of Social Psychology, 3rd ed. (New York: D. Appleton-Century Co., Inc.; 1942).

[2] Charles Bird found that only five per cent of the traits mentioned

The same heroic traits are "discovered." Likewise, the literature on "functions of the executive" attributes to him those
functions which require the very highest moral and intellectual qualities available in the organization.[3] The orthodox,
monistic conception of organization and management contains the aristocratic imagery of strong, intelligent, trustworthy, and just superiors, on the one hand; and, on the
other, the weak, inefficient, untrustworthy, and childlike
subordinates who must be closely "supervised" and "controlled."

Above we pointed out that the confusion of person and
office involved in early charisma was continued in the hierarchical status system. Many leadership studies continue this
confusion, and especially those concerned with executive

in the twenty-odd studies he analyzed were common to four or more
of these studies. *Social Psychology* (New York: D. Appleton-Century
Co., Inc.; 1940). For a summary of many more careful trait studies, see
E. DeAlton Partridge: "Leadership Among Adolescent Boys" (New
York: Teachers College, Columbia University, 1934), No. 608. Gouldner says no leadership traits have ever been found. He thinks that if the
seekers sought nonheroic qualities they might find that modern bureaucracy provides leadership opportunities for the "anal compulsives," but
very few for the receptive, contemplative, or withdrawing types. Loc.
cit., p. 39.

[3] See the summary of various statements of executive functions by
Robert Tannenbaum: "The Manager Concept: A Rational Synthesis,"
The Journal of Business of the University of Chicago, Vol. XXII (1949).
See also Chester Barnard: "Education for Executives," *The Journal of
Business*, Vol. XVIII (1945), pp. 175-82. Works on "the functions of
executives" seem to be largely disguised trait studies. "Functions" are
ascribed which could only be performed by somewhat superhuman and
heroic persons. For example, Tannenbaum says managers (1) set the
organization's purpose, (2) establish the criterion of rationality, (3)
establish the degree and type of specialization, (4) determine lines of
formal authority, (5) provide the information subordinates lack. They
also, he says, request that something be done by a specific time and give
specific orders. He says that these managerial decisions increase the
rationality of subordinate behavior, but surely this contention contains
some hidden assumptions about the quality of managers. Note that most
of his "functions" are the result of social and cultural structures and
processes. See his "Managerial Decision-Making," *J. Bus. U. Chicago*,
Vol. XXIII (1950).

traits and functions. It is automatically assumed that the appointed head is the leader. Modern social scientists are coming to the conclusion either that headship and leadership are incompatible, or that their consolidation in the same hands is very unlikely.[4] Leadership is a quality conferred upon a person by those who are lead, and in this sense the leader is always elected. An appointed person, on the other hand, must work to advance the interests of his sponsors. He cannot be a leader for his subordinates and still serve his sponsors unless there is complete harmony of interest between the two,[5] an unlikely event. In the small nonhier-

[4] See A. D. Lindsay: *The Modern Democratic State* (London: Oxford University Press; 1943); Wilbert E. Moore: *Industrial Relations and the Social Order*, rev. ed. (New York: The Macmillan Co.; 1951), p. 141; E. L. Hartley and Ruth E. Hartley: *Fundamentals of Social Psychology* (New York: Alfred A. Knopf; 1952); Robert F. Bales: "The Equilibrium Problem in Small Groups," in Talcott Parsons, Robert F. Bales, and Edward A. Shils: *Working Papers in The Theory of Action* (Glencoe, Illinois: The Free Press; 1953); Cecil A. Gibb: "Leadership," in Gardner Lindzey, ed.: *Handbook of Social Psychology* (Reading, Massachusetts: Addison-Wesley Publishing Company, Inc.; 1954), Vol. II, pp. 877-917. Even to determine who is the leader of a nonhierarchical group is very difficult and different methods of defining the leader have a very low correlation. (Ibid., p. 895.) For example, the task-orientation function and the expressive or therapeutic function require different and perhaps incompatible attitudes and roles which are rarely combined in the same person. The first function restricts and frustrates; the second binds the group together. Bales and Fiedler reached this conclusion independently. See F. E. Fiedler: "Non-Fraternization between Leaders and Followers and Its Effects on Group Productivity and Psychological Adjustment," *Proceedings of the Symposium on Preventive and Social Psychiatry*, April 15-17, 1957 (Washington, D.C.: Walter Reed Army Institute of Research; 1957); and Robert F. Bales: "Task Status and Likeability as a Function of Talking and Listening in Decision-Making Groups," in L. D. White, ed.: *The State of the Social Sciences* (Chicago: University of Chicago Press; 1956). If the leadership role relates to holding the group together (viscidity), as many have suggested, then the task-orientation function would seem to be related to formal headship and to be largely incompatible with leadership.

[5] The denial of the reality of conflict is one of the ideological necessities of bureaucracy, as we will see below. On the impossibility

archical group, there appear to be several leadership roles, and it is rare for one person to perform them all. Also, as the situation changes, the roles pass from person to person.[6] In the formally structured group, this sharing of leadership is usually impossible because of the rights of the formal superior. We conclude that far from being identical with leadership, formal headship is for the most part incompatible with the rise of leadership. However that may be, the tendency of leadership studies has been to associate heroic, charismatic traits with persons in superordinate positions; and, consequently, these studies have served an ideological purpose in helping to legitimate bureaucratic authority.[7] Fur-

---

of minority leaders exercising much leadership because of their relation to the outside world, see Norman Miller: "The Jewish Leadership of Lakeport," in Gouldner, op. cit., pp. 195-227; also Oliver C. Cox: "Leadership Among Negroes in the United States," in ibid., pp. 228-71. On the compromised position of the formal head, see Herbert A. Simon, Donald W. Smithburg and Victor A. Thompson: *Public Administration* (New York: Alfred A. Knopf; 1950), pp. 105 ff. See also Cecil A. Gibb: loc. cit.; and Moore: op. cit., pp. 141, 279-80.

[6] See Bales: "The Equilibrium Problem in Small Groups," op. cit.; Cecil A. Gibb: "The Principles and Traits of Leadership," *J. Abnorm. and Soc. Psychol.*, Vol. XLII (1947), pp. 267-84, and "Leadership," in Gardner Lindzey, ed.: op. cit., pp. 877-917. It has been found that quality of work was improved when leadership roles were widely diffused. See Sarah Mazelis: "The Relation of Role Diffusion to Work Productivity" (unpublished; 1953), listed in Lindzey, ed.: op. cit., pp. 232-3. Apparently, authority itself is not a unitary thing but composed of many elements which were scattered rather than concentrated in a single role in some primitive cultures, e.g., the Fox Indians of the Great Lakes Region. See Walter B. Miller: "Two Concepts of Authority," *The Am. Anthropologist* (April 1955). For example, among the Fox, where there was permanency of role, there was no power to direct; and where there was power to direct, there was no permanency of role.

[7] Gouldner points out that they have been ideological in another sense. They have emphasized only the leader's group-satisfying role, not his group-frustrating role. They do not emphasize oligarchy, distortion of group goals, manipulation, etc. They have sought to enhance a leader's influence over the group but not the reverse. He says, as we have been saying, that this kind of behavior is also compatible with the system of authority that channels and legitimizes leader behavior. Op. cit., pp. 48-9.

thermore, with their charismatic emphasis, leadership studies tend to keep attention focussed on individuals and not on the institutional structures that underly their difficulties and frustrations. Any potential pressure for institutional change is thereby diverted.[8]

4. *"Managerial Social Psychology"*

Leadership studies merge into the study of "management" or "supervision"—how to get the most out of employees. Both kinds of studies have been sponsored, financed, and dominated by managements, especially the latter kind.[9] Management interest in problems of co-operation is a natural outgrowth of specialization, but the resulting "managerial sociology" (or science of human relations) has performed the ideological function of diverting attention away from needs for institutional change by emphasizing the possibility of fitting the individual into the existing institutional structure. Keeping problems on the level of individuals protects the integrity of the institutional structure by presenting officials with a series of individual problems rather than with the need to revamp the whole structure and the possibly fatal admissions which that course of action implies. Thus, for example, charges of corruption in a police force are met with the statement, "If you have any evidence of some person acting corruptly, bring it to us and we will take immediate action against him."

Although modern bureaucratic organizations are, as a result of specialization, inevitably pluralistic in fact,[1] in con-

[8] We should also point out that personalizing situations provides some cognitive structuring of situations which otherwise would be too difficult to comprehend. Conversely, and by the same means, it tends to make real solutions of our problems impossible to attain.

[9] See Merton: op. cit., pp. 571-2.

[1] See Simon, Smithburg, and Thompson: op. cit., ch. xviii; and Norton E. Long: "Power and Administration," *Public Admin. Rev.*, Vol. IX (1949), pp. 257-64. On the lack of unified efficiency in a totalitarian bureaucracy, see *Fascism in Action*, H. Doc. 401, 80th Cong., 1st sess. (1947).

cept they are monocratic, monistic, monolithic structures like totalitarian states. This monocratic conception results from the hierarchical role definitions. In such structures, although conflict exists, it cannot be given legitimacy or official recognition. As March and Simon point out, the official recognition of intergroup conflict legitimizes differentiation of goals and requires bargaining processes, both of which reduce hierarchical power. They conflict with hierarchical role definitions.[2] As presently defined, bureaucratic organizations, like totalitarian states, are simply not committed to the formal resolution of intraorganizational conflict, nor to compromise.[3] Where conflict exists, it is officially denied, hidden by fictions and myths, or attributed to the individual. It is to be removed by analytic processes of discussion and counseling, reorientation and training, or by the removal of error and misconception through communication. Once all the facts are known there can be no conflict, assuming "right-thinking" or "sound" persons. If conflict persists, individuals must be remade or eliminated, because conflict attacks the legitimacy of the organization. "Smooth operations" legitimize the organization.

Bureaucracy, therefore, with its monistic system of rights, needs an ideology which denies the validity of intraorganizational conflict. "Managerial sociology" supplies this need. Whereas leadership studies have sought to replace a lost charisma and thus have served to legitimize the hierarchical positions and roles, "managerial sociology" has supplied legitimacy to the whole institutional structure. Since the individuals can be changed to fit the structure, the structure need not be changed to fit the individuals.

"Managerial sociology" is a misnomer. The basic ideas have stemmed from social psychology as well as sociology.

[2] James G. March and Herbert A. Simon: *Organizations* (New York: John Wiley & Sons, Inc.; 1958), p. 131.

[3] In a communist country, intraorganizational conflict can be due only to capitalist residues in individual consciousness, since all members of the organization must have the same *real* goal; therefore the conflict cannot legitimately be recognized. See Reinhard Bendix: *Work and Authority in Industry* (New York: John Wiley & Sons, Inc.; 1956), p. 367.

The basic objectives have been to reduce labor costs or improve output, by facilitating the adjustment of individuals, especially industrial workers, to the organization; by reducing accidents and absenteeism; and by improving morale. Recognizing the joint contributions of sociology and psychology to the system of beliefs and orientations about to be discussed, we propose to call it "managerial social psychology." [4]

From our point of view, there are three relevant tendencies in this field of research and writing. The first relates to the narrowness of the area of attention; the second to the denial of conflict; and the third to the assumption of almost infinite manipulability of people. We will discuss them in that order.

Sociopsychological studies of organizations have been largely concerned with problems as defined by management. This concern is understandable since management finances these studies. Emphasis on morale and output have concentrated attention on the conditions of work, first physical and now social. [5] Harold Lasswell has pointed out that

[4] Almost anything we say about this body of writing and research will do injustice to specific individuals, and for this we apologize in advance. Nevertheless, certain ideological tendencies of the field as a whole are clearly visible, and these are the tendencies we propose to discuss. For other criticisms of "managerial sociology," see Wilbert E. Moore: "Current Issues in Industrial Sociology," *Am. Sociol. Rev.*, Vol. XII, pp. 651-7; Reinhard Bendix and Lloyd H. Fisher: "The Perspectives of Elton Mayo," *Rev. Economics and Statistics*, Vol. XXXI, pp. 312-19; C. Wright Mills: "The Contributions of Sociology to Studies of Industrial Relations," *Industrial Relations Research Association, Proceedings 1948*, Publication No. 1 (Urbana, Illinois: Industrial Relations Research Association, 1949), pp. 199-222; Morton Grodzins: "Public Administration and the Science of Human Relations," *Public Admin. Rev.*, Vol. IX (1951), pp. 88-102.

[5] Examples of this approach are, Elton Mayo: *Human Problems of an Industrial Civilization* (New York: The Macmillan Co.; 1933); Fritz J. Roethlisberger: *Management and Morale* (Cambridge: Harvard University Press; 1941); F. J. Roethlisberger and William J. Dickson. *Management and the Worker* (Cambridge: Harvard University Press; 1939), and Thomas N. Whitehead: *The Industrial Worker* (Cambridge: Harvard University Press; 1938).

this "contented cow" approach restricts attention to areas much narrower than the "zones of activity" which most vitally affect employees' fate.[6] While affairs at the bottom of the hierarchy are illuminated in almost blinding fashion, this illumination recedes as we proceed up the hierarchy, leaving the very top in almost total darkness except for an occasional stockholder's suit, antitrust suit, or legislative investigation.[7] The net result of this bias is to obscure the institutional setting within which work takes place. In a sense, modern bureaucratic theory is an attempt to supply what has been missing, but it suffers seriously from lack of empirical data.

"Managerial social psychology" tends to deny the validity of intraorganizational conflict. Conflict is regarded as a form of aberrant individual behavior to be corrected by working on or with individual employees and their working-group environment. This "aberrant" behavior is attacked in four principal ways. First, on the assumption that conflict would not occur if the individual were properly integrated into a "democratic" group,[8] efforts are made to improve the human relations of the work situation and to facilitate the formation of primary groups of identifying people. It has been pointed out that the term "democratic" as applied to groups or practices in this literature does not have the usual connotations.[9] Rather, it means a structured group characterized by

[6] Harold Lasswell: *Power and Personality* (New York: W. W. Norton & Company, Inc.; 1948), p. 193. See also Delbert C. Miller and William H. Form: *Industrial Sociology* (New York: Harper & Brothers; 1951), pp. 74-7.

[7] See Gouldner: op. cit., pp. 47-9.

[8] In addition to the citations in ft. nt. 5, above, see Kurt Lewin: *Resolving Social Conflicts* (New York: Harper & Brothers; 1948), and "The Practicality of Democracy," in Gardner Murphy, ed.: *Human Nature and Enduring Peace* (Boston: Houghton Mifflin Co.; 1945); Albert D. Annis and Norman C. Meier: "The Induction of Opinion through Suggestion By Means of Planted Content," *J. Soc. Psychol.*, Vol. V (1934), pp. 65-81; K. Dunker: "Experimental Modification of Children's Food Preferences through Social Suggestion," *J. Abnorm. and Soc. Psychol.*, Vol. XXXIII (1938), pp. 489-507.

[9] See Henry S. Kariel: "Democracy Unlimited: Kurt Lewin's Field Theory," *Am. J. Sociol.*, Vol. LXII (1956), pp. 280-9. Kariel

paternalism; the formal superior uses his superordinate rights with humanitarian and liberal restraint.[1]

The emphasis upon individual integration into the democratic group leads to a second emphasis upon the development of democratic leadership skills. The assumption here is that conflict may be a result of inadequate leadership skills. A science of human manipulation develops[2] and along with it a veritable deluge of "executive development" and "supervisory training" programs, and evening courses in "conference leadership."

Related to the emphasis on development of leadership skills is the growing emphasis on the skills of communication. Here the assumption is that conflict arises because of failure to grasp the whole situation, itself a failure of communication by those around one, especially one's superiors. If all people in a given situation had the same perception of the situation, there could be no conflict. The result of this assumption has been the rapid growth of training in communication skills, both within bureaucracies and within the schools. The further realization that perception of the situation of action is socially conditioned, and is to some extent a function of one's attitudes and social role, has led to attempts to increase the individual's insight into himself and others. Conflict may be simply a result of inability to put oneself in another's place. A great training apparatus has

quotes Otto Klineberg's conclusions from group dynamics experiments as follows: "the more 'democratic' the procedures, the less resistance there is to change, and the greater the productivity." Otto Klineberg: *Social Psychology* (New York: Holt, Rinehart and Winston, Inc.; 1954), p. 464, in loc. cit., p. 286, ft. nt. 27.

[1] For the easy integration of democratic and hierarchical concepts in this literature, see Ronald Lippitt: *Training in Community Relations* (New York: Harper & Brothers; 1949) especially p. 144; and Lewin: "The Practicality of Democracy," in op. cit.

[2] See for example, Alex Bavelas: "Morale and the Training of Leaders," in Goodwin Watson, ed.: *Civilian Morale* (Boston: Houghton Mifflin Co.; 1942), pp. 143-65; Morris S. Viteles: *Motivation and Morale in Industry* (New York: W. W. Norton & Company, Inc.; 1953); and William C. Schutz: "The Interpersonal Underworld," *Harvard Business Review* (July-August 1958), pp. 123-35.

been developed to increase these social skills of insight into oneself and others, called psychodrama, wherein individuals exchange roles for play-acting training sessions.[3]

In summary, this field of thought and research holds that conflict is not objectively real or valid. It is a subjective experience of the individual and arises because he is not properly integrated into the group under skillful leadership, where adequate communication and social participation would dispel erroneous perceptions of reality.

A third ideological tendency of "managerial social psychology" is based upon its assumption that people are almost infinitely manipulable.[4] Of course, anyone nowadays who argues that man is a completely unpredictable creature who cannot be influenced in any predictable direction is whistling into the wind. There are, however, some very practical limits to such influence, or "control" as it is often hopefully termed. To reorient behavior in any particular direction may require adjustments of values and rewards; and the direction-defining group, the "management" in bureaucracy, may be unwilling to make these adjustments. Managerial social psychology accepts the norms of management and seeks to manipulate employees in the direction of those

[3] See Gustav Ichheiser: "Misunderstanding in Human Relations: A Study in False Social Perception," *Am. J. Sociol.*, Vol. LV (1949), Part Two; Gardner Murphy: "The Role of Psychologists in the Establishment of Better Human Relations," in Lyman Bryson, *et al.*, eds.: *Perspectives on a Troubled Decade* (New York: Harper & Brothers; 1950), pp. 1-11; Dorwin Cartwright: "Achieving Change in People: Some Applications of Group Dynamics Theory," *Human Relations*, Vol. IV (1951), pp. 381-93; Carl I. Hovland: "Changes in Attitude through Communication," *J. Abnorm. and Soc. Psychol.*, Vol. XLVI (1951), pp. 424-37; and Dorwin Cartwright: *The Research Center for Group Dynamics: A Report of Five Years' Activities and a View of Future Needs* (Ann Arbor: Institute for Social Research, University of Michigan; 1950).

[4] "If we can but discover . . . those laws whereby a given 'life-space' inevitably produces a given behavior, then we can know how to change persons and groups to remake their behavior according to our hearts' desires." Edward C. Tolman: "Kurt Lewin—1890-1947," *J. Soc. Issues*, Vol. VI, Suppl. Ser. No. 1 (1948) pp. 22-6; p. 23 quoted by Kariel: loc. cit., p. 284.

norms. Although many practitioners of the new art are becoming convinced that a more or less fundamental change in management values is a prerequisite to bureaucratic harmony, we think it not unfair to say that theoretical formulations in this field accept management norms as given. Consequently, whereas the individual could undoubtedly be "manipulated" or "changed" by a change in hierarchical values, such a change is not seriously proposed; it would attack the institution of hierarchy. Instead, it is alleged, Rousseau-fashion, that a right-thinking individual will achieve harmony with his environment.[5]

An enormous bias discloses itself at this point, for why is "right-thinking" restricted to only one side of the conflict? The answer is that the institutional distribution of rights has been put not only beyond criticism but beyond imagination. Consequently, the management of conflict, both in theory and organizational practice, is repressive. Attention is diverted away from the development of formal bases and devices for settling conflict. The repression of conflict eliminates only its appearance, resulting in false harmony.[6]

[5] "The discrepancy between what people 'should do, if they were guided by their real interest,' and what they actually do is frequently caused by the fact that a person feels himself belonging to those to whom he is similar or to whom he wishes to be similar. On the other hand, his 'real interest' would demand that he should feel belonging to those upon whom his dependence is greatest." Kurt Lewin: "Field Theory and Experiment in Social Psychology: Concepts and Methods," *Am. J. Sociol.*, Vol. XLIV (1939), pp. 887 (quoted), 868-96. Quoted by Kariel: loc. cit., p. 284.

[6] Fromm argues that psychiatry and psychoanalysis as practiced in our society are also repressive, for much the same reason—the refusal to admit an institutional source of frustrations. *Escape From Freedom* (New York: Holt, Rinehart and Winston, Inc.; 1941), p. 246. The denial of conflict results in repression of affective communication. Leavit has pointed out that this repression results in failure to communicate fact, as well as affect. (Op. cit., p. 214.) In fact, such repression probably has its principal effects upon the cognitive rather than the affective system in an organization. It has been shown that even where almost complete breaks in cognitive communication occur, affective communication will still take place. See William Caudill: *The Psychi-*

5. *Responsibility*

Thus far in this chapter we have discussed ideological support given to the hierarchical institution by leadership studies and managerial social psychology. One other system of ideas is important in protecting hierarchical legitimacy. We refer to the formal concept of bureaucratic responsibility.

The monistic formulation states that each individual in an organization receives his right to act from his superior and is responsible to his superior for the manner in which he uses that right. He in turn delegates authority to his subordinates, and they are similarly responsible to him, etc. Even though functions are increasingly lost to specialists and authority to act must consequently be delegated, it is stated that the superior "still has the responsibility" for the actions taken.[7] Though specialists actually do the work, the executive has the right, or the "responsibility," to do it. This use of the term seems to be partly a vindicative justification of a position which has lost or is losing functions to specialists.[8] As used in this way, the term "responsibility" *denotes* authority, the right to make personnel changes, organizational changes, policy changes, etc.; but it suggests or *connotes* duty, therefore blamability. This connotation is the ideological element.

Above we have suggested the existence of a confusion between responsibility as *right*, or competency, or jurisdic-

---

atric Hospital as a Small Society (Cambridge: Harvard University Press; 1958).

[7] It is hardly necessary to document this statement, but nevertheless see Moore: *Industrial Relations and The Social Order*, p. 124. Discussing change he says it "is the special function of technical specialists who stand in an advisory capacity to the executive. *But the responsibility* for decision as to changes . . . rests with the executive." Almost as many similar statements could be found as there are books on the subject.

[8] Harold Leavitt makes essentially the same point. Op. cit., pp. 156-0.

tion, and responsibility as duty, or blamability, and creditability. However, it does not seem that blame or credit are appropriate to rights. We may credit a person for doing well, but only on the assumption that he should do so.[9] Conversely, we blame him for not doing well only on the assumption that he should do well, that he has a duty to do well. If "responsibility" is used in the first sense, as right, or authority, the central postulate of the monistic theory of responsibility, namely, that "authority should be commensurate with responsibility," means that authority should be commensurate with authority, a tautology. This same postulate, if "responsibility" is interpreted in the second sense as blamability, means that right or jurisdiction or authority should equal liability for blame. But one is liable for blame in connection with his duty, not his rights; and so rights and blamability are not even comeasurable, let alone equal. The statement should read, therefore, liability for blame should equal duty. But a person's duty in the monistic theory is exhausted in his duty to his superior. The central postulate of the monistic concept of responsibility, therefore, appears to be only a restatement of hierarchical role relations as culturally defined and of the rights and duties of which those relations are constituted.

Blame or credit for the outcome of events implicitly assumes or alleges some ability to influence the outcome. As we have seen, specialization reduces any one person's ability so to influence events, tending to make responsibility, as blame or credit, either unjust or ritualistic. From this point of view, authority equal to responsibility could mean ability, or power over events, equal to blamability, or hierarchical duty. But ability cannot be bestowed, and so the postulate may counsel a reduction of liability for blame (but probably not credit); or it could indicate a desire for actual authority, as rights or jurisdiction, equal to expected responsibility, considered as rights or jurisdiction. "My au-

---

[9] Even to credit a person because he did what he tried to do suggests that he *ought* to do what he tries to do. More often we credit a person for doing what he ought to do, which means that he started off from duty rather than right.

thority should be as large as I think it should be." Division chiefs, for example, grumble because they do not have authority over recruitment or purchasing for "their" division.

As discussed in a previous chapter, discrepancies between actual authority and expected authority can arise because authority can be delegated to defined, nonhierarchical competencies either through centralizations impelled by advancing specialization or through acts of power. Since the conception of the proper authority of a hierarchical position is culturally defined, and nonhierarchical authority is organizationally defined, a person in any hierarchical position is likely to find that his actual authority is not commensurate with his expected authority. The central postulate could be restated: "Actual authority should be commensurate with expected authority." [1]

The monistic concept of responsibility is not as simple as it is often made to sound. If a person is blamed for or credited with acts of his subordinates beyond or contrary to his instructions, his hierarchical rights are transposed into duties. The definition of his relation to his subordinates is exhausted in the definition of his relation to his superior. If his subordinates achieve the hierarchically given goal "X" by disregarding his commands or authority, and he is credited, his authority is being treated as irrelevant; similarly, his authority is being treated as irrelevant if his correct commands for achieving goal "X" are disregarded by his subordinates and he is blamed for the resulting failure. The same considerations apply, even more so, to insubordinate acts several levels below a person and for which he is blamed by his superior.

The destructive impact on hierarchical rights which the monistic theory of responsibility would have if it were followed literally is even more apparent when we consider blame for events in connection with the *ability* to influence them, rather than only the *right* to do so. If a person is

[1] Since there is no way to protect actual authority from the advance of specialization, role conceptions are protected somewhat by hiding the discrepancy between the actual and the expected by means of fictions and "just pretend" behavior. See the next chapter.

blamed or credited for events or outcomes which he could not influence, he is treated, morally, as a nonperson, something without rights. Morally he could be defined as a general duty to absorb blame or credit. Such is responsibility in the purely ritualistic form of the scapegoat.

However, if the subordinates' behavior is considered to be determined by the superior, as the monistic theory suggests when it states that the superior tells subordinates what to do (organizes) and how to do it (supervises), to blame the superior for subordinate acts becomes more intelligible. "Responsibility," as suggestive of the superior's blamability for subordinate acts, tends to protect the hierarchical role definitions. Logically, however, this idea of responsibility ends in a nullity because, under the monistic theory, the superior's behavior is determined by *his* superior, etc., leaving the former blameless.

Consequently, regardless of its connotation, with its ideological implications, "responsibility" for subordinates' actions, in monistic theory, is not "responsibility" as blamability. Since, as we have seen, the term as here used cannot logically mean either right ("authority should be commensurate with authority") or blamability, we must find another meaning for the term as used in the proposition that the superior is responsible for subordinates' actions. We suggest that what is meant by this proposition in practice is that inquiries and replies concerning subordinates' actions are routed through formal channels, hence the office of the superior. This routing of inquiries and replies is what is meant by accountability. The superior accounts (describes, explains, reports) for subordinates' actions to *his* superior. If the replies are not satisfactory, so that blame is indicated, the formal theory does not tell us who *should* be blamed but *suggests* that the superior *is* blamed.

When the term "responsibility" is used in this sense, the central postulate of the concept of responsibility should read: "Jurisdiction, or authority, should be commensurate with communication about the jurisdiction, or with accountability." Since much will be inquired about which the superior could not influence, his responsibility, as accountability, will always be greater than his ability, or power to affect outcomes; and also increasingly greater than his authority, or jurisdiction, because of increasing specialist influence on his subordinates from centralized "staff" sources.[2]

Responsibility as blamability is more than a normative theory. There is the *fact* of blame. The halo provided by the status system makes blame increasingly difficult as we go up the hierarchy. Very high positions become immune.[3]

People praise a god but do not blame him, not because of any doubts as to his complete control of events but precisely because of his possession of this power. Not only are they afraid to blame, but they also feel that it would be *lèse majesté* ("sacrilegious," in religious terms) because of his high status. The more powerless a person is in terms of reprisal potential, the easier it is to blame him. Hierarchical positions have reprisal power in terms of personal goals and so cannot be easily blamed by persons occupying positions lower in the system. As to blame from above, the status system tends to suppress blame, even as it skews the distribution of credit. Blame would undermine the legitimacy of the system.[4] Furthermore, as we point out in the next chapter, high-status persons constitute a carefully selected

[2] The term "responsibility" is also used as a synonym for discretion. The "responsible" person is one who acts so as to protect and promote the values of a group of which he is a member in his encounters with outgroups or events. See Selznick: *TVA and the Grass Roots* (Berkeley: University of California Press; 1949), pp. 211-12. As used in this sense, "responsibility" is a combination of loyalty and craftiness. Chester Barnard uses the term essentially in this sense. *The Functions of the Executive* (Cambridge: Harvard University Press; 1938), p. 269.

[3] Barnard points out that very high-status people are hard to get rid of and consequently must often be "kicked upstairs." See "Functions and Pathology of Status Systems in Formal Organizations," in *The Functions of the Executive.*

[4] See Arthur K. Davis: "Bureaucratic Patterns in the Navy Officer Corps," *Social Forces*, Vol. XXVII (1948), pp. 143-53. As he says, "This may help us to understand the reluctance of military systems to punish their officers. A public trial is a threat to the charisma of the uniform and to the whole structure of authority, because it destroys the basic premise that the king will do no wrong."

team, and the integrity of the team must be protected by protecting each member of it. It is also true that the rights and powers of high-status positions give the incumbents much greater means of self-defense. Furthermore, despite fictions and dramaturgy, it is becoming apparent that persons in the higher superordinate positions do not and cannot in fact have much influence on the course of events. The tendency, therefore, is to find the actual culprit, the person whose initials indicate that he dictated the memo for the boss's signature; the person who actually gave the advice; etc.[5]

---

[5] Note the approach of Congressional Committees when they discover administrative actions of which they disapprove. They often ask the Department for a "full history" of the case as well as a list of "those who persuaded the Department not to act." The words are those of Robert Kennedy, Counsel to the Senate Rackets Committee, on December 4, 1958, in regard to a reputed mobster who was allowed by the Internal Revenue Service to make up for failing to file an income tax return for seven years while he was hiding out in Ohio. (Reported in the *Chicago Sun-Times*, December 5, 1958.) In December, 1958, a fire in a Chicago parochial school took over 90 lives. No one was blamed, but intensive efforts were made to find two boys who were alleged to have smoked cigarettes in the stairwell, where the fire originated, shortly before it began. In the previous year, a newspaper discovered that an out-of-state insurance company paid $35,000 to a lobbyist to influence legislation in Illinois that would save the company $50,000 a year. When this story broke, the board of directors of the company convened and publicly put all the blame on a low-level government man. His punishment was that he was not allowed to contact government officials for some time. In the Nuremberg War Trials, individuals were not allowed to plead the orders of superiors as a defense. See *The Case Against The Nazi War Criminals* by Robert H. Jackson (New York: Alfred A. Knopf; 1946).

In corporate crime, even when a corporation is convicted, the officers are usually acquitted. See Edwin H. Sutherland: *White Collar Crime* (New York: The Dryden Press; 1949).

The penal sanctions of the Sherman Act are seldom used and then almost always against labor unionists and racketeers. Jack W. Peltason and James M. Burns, eds.: *Functions and Policies of American Government* (Englewood Cliffs, New Jersey: Prentice-Hall, Inc.; 1958), p. 258.

Life Magazine has carefully explained why specialization of activities and interests in television makes it impossible to pin down responsi-

Because of the difficulty of blaming high-status persons and the ease of blaming people with little reprisal potential, and because of the tendency to try to find the actual culprit, blame shifts to the lower regions of organizations. For the same reasons, the outcomes selected for formal blame tend to be the rather inconsequential ones. Those individuals who can and sometimes do "give the country away" are rarely stuck with the consequences of their acts. It is usually for their peccadillos that they are castigated.

Apparently, people achieve cognitive stability by associating individuals and events in a single, cognitive unit. Whether naive or sophisticated, theories of responsibility as blamability are the result. To primitive people, any connection between a person and an event gives rise to responsibility claims.[6] Sophistication with regard to imputations of responsibility gradually increases as society ascends from the primitive state. A person would be responsible if he were a necessary condition of the event, regardless of his intentions. Later, a person would be held to be responsible if he were a necessary condition and could foresee the outcome, regardless of his intentions. Still later, he must have intended it as well. Today, we are beginning to realize that even his intentions may partly depend upon his environment, possibly excusing him from responsibility (note insanity pleas and the importance attached to premeditation in criminal law). The monistic theory of responsibility as blamability rests at the most primitive level. There a person is responsible even though he could not foresee the out-

bility for the unhappy state of affairs in that beleaguered industry. (November 16, 1959), pp. 32-3. The rapid footwork of top managements in avoiding any responsibility (blame) for rigged bidding and price-fixing in the electrical equipment industry, and the fixing of blame (but no organizational punishment) on lower-level scapegoats, was one of the most interesting aspects of the recent travails of that industry.

The vague and tenuous connection of the high-status person with events makes it easy to absolve him from blame.

[6] The following ideas are from Fritz Heider. See "Social Perception and Phenomenal Causality," *Psychol. Rev.*, Vol. LI (1949), pp. 358-74, and "Attitudes and Cognitive Organization," *J. Psychol.*, Vol. XXI (1946), pp. 107-12.

come, was not a necessary condition, and did not intend it. If this theory were usually applied, responsibility in our organizations would be largely a ritualistic performance of the ancient institution of the scapegoat enacted by the hierarchy. Nothing could be further from reality than to depict the bureaucratic hierarchy as an institutionalized system of scapegoats. The fact is, that the monistic theory of responsibility is not only a simple intellectual confusion, but also part of the ideological apparatus by which hierarchical roles are protected. The emphasis, often by connotation rather than denotation, upon responsibility as blamability is charismatic. It projects the image of the hero standing between his people and blame or punishment ("He died to atone for our sins"). For simple people, ambivalence toward the charismatic leader, their love and fear, or hate, of him[7] is given a cognitive structure in the formal theory of responsibility. His is the credit and the love, the blame and the hate.

The imputation of responsibility protects and increases the superior's authority. Since he "gets the blame," his subordinates should do whatever he says. Furthermore, the belief that the superior's blame is greater tends to legitimate his greater power, status, and privileges.[8]

For the concept of responsibility to function ideologically in defense of hierarchical roles, it must be denied as a device for the protection of specialist roles. Both within organizations and during their formal schooling, many technical specialists are taught to view responsibility as a hierarchical, or "administrative," function. Theirs is only to point out, from the basis of their technical knowledge, the technical or specialist implications of proposals.[9] "Responsibility" as an ideological device belongs to hierarchy. Since,

---

[7] See David Krech and Richard S. Crutchfield: *Theory and Problems of Social Psychology* (New York: McGraw-Hill Book Co.; 1948), especially p. 421.

[8] We should point out that the monistic concept, by defining the superior as the responsible party, defines the subordinates as *not* responsible ("irresponsible"?). Thus, there is a peculiar irony in the widespread contention of supervisors that their subordinates are unwilling to take responsibility.

[9] Merton: op. cit., chs. vii, xii.

as we have seen, the monistic theory of hierarchical responsibility does not and could not correspond to practice, it is obviously necessary to control the flow of information about reality. It is necessary to control impressions about hierarchical positions and the roles related thereto. In the next chapter we discuss this dramaturgical approach to role defense.

CHAPTER 7

Dramaturgy

1. The Dramaturgical Aspect of Organizations

In a remarkable study, Erving Goffman has recently shown how the performance of their roles of various kinds involves people in impression management.[1] We must try to control the information or cues imparted to others in order to protect our representations of self and to control the impressions others form about us. We are all involved, therefore, in dramaturgy.

Although, for reasons given below, this chapter is principally concerned with dramaturgy in the hierarchy, we should mention briefly that specialization also has its dramaturgical side. Specialist dramaturgy seems to be particularly related to the problem of accreditation. The ubiquitous white coat of the medical doctor suggests that here is a man of fastidious cleanliness, the stethoscope dangling from his pocket suggests the great and mysterious range of his knowledge. The engineer's slide rule performs a similar function.

[1] Erving Goffman: *The Presentation of Self in Everyday Life* (Garden City, New York: Doubleday & Company, Inc.; 1959).

If a specialist role is only weakly established, we should expect a dramaturgy of insecurity, with pompous self-importance, lack of communicativeness, etc.

As Goffman points out, the dramaturgical side of formal organizations has been neglected. Students have in the past been interested in the technical, the political, the structural, and the cultural aspects, but not this.[2] We believe that dramaturgical behavior in the bureaucratic organization is structurally related to its other and more familiar characteristics. Perceptions of leadership, status, and power depend heavily upon communication.[3] People will rate a position in a scale of leadership, status, or power at least partly in accordance with information they have about that position. The control of information, therefore, and the management of impressions, become important techniques in the struggle for authority, status, and power.

2. Legitimation of Authority Roles

We have argued throughout this book that a number of developments are challenging the legitimacy of hierarchical authority in bureaucratic organization. Particularly crucial is the gap which advancing specialization and technical complexity are creating between the right to take a specific action and the knowledge needed to do so. Cultural definitions of hierarchical rights and expectations of hierarchical role performance are increasingly at war with reality. The greater the discrepancy between the self-image projected, on the

[2] Ibid., pp. 239-40.
[3] See Robert F. Bales: "The Equilibrium Problem in Small Groups," in Talcott Parsons, Robert F. Bales, and Edward A. Shils: *Working Papers in The Theory of Action* (Glencoe, Illinois: The Free Press; 1953); Cecil A. Gibb: "Leadership," in Gardner Lindzey, ed.: *Handbook of Social Psychology* (Reading, Massachusetts: Addison-Wesley Publishing Company, Inc.; 1954) and the discusssion of status ranking above in ch. iv. That perceptions of power may be dramaturgically manipulated is clearly indicated in John W. Thibaut and Harold H. Kelley: *The Social Psychology of Groups* (New York: John Wiley & Sons, Inc.; 1959), pp. 122-4.

one hand, and reality, on the other, the greater the load placed upon sheer play acting. Dramaturgical skill has become increasingly essential to the hierarchical role, and technical competence increasingly irrelevant.[4]

Discrepancies between role expectations and the technical imperatives related to goal accomplishment are generally hidden or at least disguised by fictions, myths, and "just-pretend" behavior which are quite general throughout our bureaucratic organizations. For instance, the inability of the organization to live with the superior's right to control communication leads inevitably to the development of elaborate informal channels of communication. The existence of these informal channels is often officially denied, or the superior's signature is put on the communication by rubber stamp to pretend that it came from him.[5] If these informal

[4] See Alvin W. Gouldner: *Studies in Leadership: Leadership and Democratic Action* (New York: Harper & Brothers; 1950), pp. 225-7. This statement refers only to the hierarchical aspect of any particular job, not its specialist aspect; however, as we have repeatedly stated, the specialist content becomes more and more attenuated as one goes up the hierarchy. "We sit at our desks all day," says a business chief executive, "while around us whiz and gyrate a vast number of special activities, some of which we only dimly understand. And for each of these activities there is a specialist. . . . But it has reached a point where the greatest task of the president is to understand enough of all these specialties so that when a problem comes up he can assign the right team of experts to work on it." John L. McCaffrey: "What Corporation Presidents Think about at Night," *Fortune* (September 1953), pp. 128 ff., quoted in C. Wright Mills: *The Power Elite* (New York: Oxford University Press, Inc.; 1957), p. 135.

The extent to which "management" has been specialized out of executive (management) positions can be illustrated by the special subjects discussed at an industrial management conference at Illinois Institute of Technology on February 5 and 6, 1959. The subjects included sales forecasts, preparing budgets, quality control, cost considerations, engineering economics, launching a new product, market surveys, wage incentives, operations research, data processing, new site selection, human engineering, production and inventory planning, automation, research and development expenditures, and new product selection. See the references in ch. viii, pp. 156-7, ft. nt. 8.

[5] The signature also acts as a surety that the source will not refuse to acknowledge the communication later.

channels are depicted on organizational charts (they usually are not), dotted lines are used, indicating the taint of illegality about them. In general, any informal or unofficial arrangements are considered somewhat illegal and are undertaken surreptitiously.

The fact that those who are traditionally empowered to make all decisions cannot any longer have the range of knowledge necessary to do so brings about a good deal of pretense in organizational activities. In fact, much of the organization's work is done by surreptitious methods. Everyone is involved in "playing the game." Reality is hidden by "double talk." As Goffman points out,[6] "double-talk" communication may convey information between people inconsistent with their roles. One person in a relationship says one thing but means something else. The overt expression is consistent with the formal relationship, but the hidden meaning is not. The other person in the relationship may accept the hidden communication; or he may ignore it and accept the overt expression which is consistent with the relationship, which is "proper." A common example concerns breaking in a new boss. When an assistant must break in a new boss, he will have to convey instructions to his boss in a form which makes it appear overtly as though he were receiving these instructions from the boss. This kind of communication occurs in connection with matters outside a person's formal jurisdiction but depending upon him. It occurs when a subordinate tries to seize the direction of action or his superior tries to extend it to him. In this kind of situation, "double-talk" communication allows a subordinate to initiate lines of endeavor without giving explicit recognition to the implications this action has for the formal role relationship between him and his superior.[7]

[6] Op. cit., pp. 194-5.

[7] As Whyte says about junior subordinates: "Given minimum committeemanship skills, by an adroit question here and a modest suggestion there, he can call attention to himself and *still play the game.*" *The Organization Man* (Garden City, New York: Doubleday & Company, Inc.; 1957), p. 168 (my italics). There is sometimes a special problem in presenting the results of work to others outside the unit. The

Discrepancies between actual authority and expected authority inevitably arise, because organizationally defined competencies of centralized specialties conflict with the culturally defined rights of hierarchical position. The attempt is universally made to hide these discrepancies by simply denying them. Thus it is alleged that the central specialists, the "staff," only advise; they have no authority. If their advice comes in the form of a command, everyone is supposed to pretend that it comes from a higher executive, and sometimes provision is made to have his signature stamped on the more formal specialist commands. This "just-pretend" behavior also protects status-inflated self-images of those receiving specialist commands, a necessity since these commands are quite likely to come from lower-status people.[8]

The dramaturgical management of impressions about hierarchical positions and roles is no longer a sporadic affair depending upon the accidents of personality. It appears to be institutionally organized. That is to say, opportunities for hierarchical success in modern bureaucracy depend to a very large extent upon the ability and willingness to engage in impression management. Our contention is that this kind of behavior is essential as a device for maintaining the legitimacy of hierarchical roles in the face of advancing specialization. Although no leadership traits have been discovered, a definite executive type seems to be emerging.[9]

---

superior's rights of communication and his claim of responsibility require that he make the presentation. Since he is less familiar with it than the others, a rather intricate business of prompting is often required. (Goffman refers to "staging cues"). Sign language and other secret communicative devices are then used, such as foot scraping, voice clearing, fidgeting, etc. See Goffman: op. cit., p. 185; also Victor A. Thompson: *The Regulatory Process in OPA Rationing* (New York: King's Crown Press; 1950), p. 311. See also Peter B. Hammond: "The Function of Indirection in Communication," in *Comparative Studies in Administration*, edited by the Staff of the Administrative Science Center, University of Pittsburgh (University of Pittsburgh Press; 1959).

[8] See above, ch. iii.

[9] It has been reported that employers now seem to look for an ideal "Hollywood type." Perrin Stryker, quoting Ann Hoff, the placement expert: "How Executives Get Jobs," *Fortune* (August 1953),

3. *Dramaturgy of the Superior*

What are the impressions fostered by hierarchical dramaturgy? As would be expected, they are the heroic and charismatic qualities—the same ones that leadership-trait studies have been seeking. The impression is fostered that occupants of hierarchical positions are, of all people in the organization, the ablest, the most industrious, the most indispensable, the most loyal, the most reliable, the most self-controlled, the most ethical, which is to say, the most honest, fair, and impartial. Technical skill is not among these fostered impressions. Modern bureaucracy derogates technical skill or any great learning. To "get ahead," a person must give up his technical specialty.[1] By derogating the role of the specialist, the superior protects his own role in the hierarchy.

It is within this framework that the extreme busyness of persons in hierarchical positions is to be understood. Busyness suggests indispensability, as Riesman, Glazer, and Denney[2] have noted. It also suggests that the very busy per

---

p. 182. Shape of teeth and size of ears have disqualified men. (Ibid.) ". . . executives often project an air of competency and general grasp of the situation." Goffman: op. cit., p. 47. "More and more, the executive must act according to the role that he is cast for—the calm eye that never strays from the other's gaze, the easy, controlled laughter, the whole demeanor that tells onlookers that here certainly is a man without neurosis and inner rumblings," Whyte: op. cit., p. 172. For an essentially similar but somewhat unfriendly characterization, see Mills: op. cit., pp. 142-3.

[1] See ch. v and the references there cited on p. 98 in ft. nt. 5.

[2] David Riesman, Nathan Glazer, and Reuel Denney: *The Lonely Crowd* (Garden City, New York: Doubleday & Company, Inc.; 1953), pp. 307-8. Note that questions of how much "work" a person does, of "overwork," of reimbursable work are matters of cultural definition. Thus, for example, the work of the housewife is not so defined, and so she is tired out at night, yet suffers a sense of guilt for "having done nothing" all day, while her "overworked" husband is entitled to the children's and her sympathy when he comes home at night. (Ibid., pp. 300, 308.) People generally do not think of the long hours of the scientist in his lab or the writer at his desk as being "overwork." The

son is of unusual importance to the organization and takes its interests more to heart than do others. The very busy person is felt to be more dependable and loyal than the others. Consequently, it is advisable for those who want to get ahead to load their briefcases when they leave at night, and perhaps to come in for a few hours on the week end.[3]

Impression management follows certain broad rules already supplied by the culture. Such audience rules as taking a person at his face value and not interfering with his performance when it is going on operate to everyone's advantage. Persons in high positions have some additional dramaturgical advantages in the form of hierarchical rights, especially their rights to deference. The status system is sustained by its own well worn dramaturgical apparatus, including familiar status symbols such as insignia, titles, and ceremonies; and office symbols such as private offices, rugs, and special furniture. "A name on the door rates a rug on the floor." [4]

Impression management requires that some attention be paid to the preparation of the audience.[5] For hierarchical presentations, the audience has already been prepared by the status system. The audience is trained to take cues at their face value, to show the proper appreciation for the performance. Status behavior protects the backstage area by teaching people to "keep their place." Information inconsistent with fostered impressions is kept secret. Status training has pre-

---

specialist who spends his evenings reading works in the field of his special interest is not considered to have taken work home from the office. Then, of course, there is always the question of the usefulness of activities. One good idea may be much more valuable in relation to organizational goals than large amounts of *pro forma* memo writing or conference, board, or committee attendance. When the end result of activities is not a countable pile of objects, it is probably impossible to determine who works the "hardest," and the brilliant person may accomplish more with apparently less "work" than the less brilliant.

[3] See Whyte: op. cit., p. 158.

[4] See Chester Barnard: "Functions and Pathology of Status Systems in Formal Organizations," In William Foote Whyte, ed.: *Industry and Society* (New York: McGraw-Hill Book Co.; 1946); also Thompson: op. cit., p. 323.

[5] Goffman: op. cit., ch. vi.

pared the audience to exercise tact, and the performers to exercise tact with respect to tact. Both sides "play the game," thus protecting the performances from miscues, bad acting, *faux pas*, "scenes," etc.

An act has a better chance of coming off well when the audience is not too large and when the interaction is of short duration.[6] Superiors are therefore admonished to deal with subordinates individually and privately. The status system allows the hierarchical superior to choose his audience, the time, place, and duration of the performance, by giving the high-status person the initiative in interaction. He can usually begin and terminate the interview. This ability to control the timing of the interaction is particularly valuable in sustaining the impression of busyness and importance to the organization.[7]

The more background information possessed by the audience, the less likely it is that the performance will have an important influence.[8] The status system puts social distance between people so that the audience is not likely to have much background information about higher-status performers. Superiors are therefore advised not to become intimate with subordinates. "Don't go to lunch with the wrong person." The executive eats in an "executive dining room"; he has a private secretary disciplined in discretion; he has control of access to his office.[9] Finally, the status system provides a more or less elaborate set of staging devices or props as background for the management of impressions about the character and activities of persons occupying hierarchical roles.[1]

[6] Ibid.

[7] See Thompson: op. cit., pp. 324-5. Modern bureaucratic telephone technique can be at least partly understood as a dramaturgical competition between two secretaries to see which can force the other's boss to come on the line first, thereby having to wait until the "busier" one is plugged in. Ibid., p. 323.

[8] Goffman: op. cit.

[9] Thus an executive can make a graceful gesture by instituting an "open door" policy, safe in the assurance that the status system will protect access to his office almost as well as a locked door.

[1] We refer to the symbols which make the status visible, discussed

The point has been made that the general institutionalized system of deference, the "status system," provides a
set of situational definitions of great value for the management of impressions on the part of persons in the hierarchy.
Other general attitudes toward self-expression reinforce the
status system in this respect. People generally believe there
is a "sacred compatibility between the man and the job," [2] a
sacred connection between the right to play a part and the
capacity to do so. Since the person in a hierarchical position
has the right to make "decisions," he is assumed to have the
ability to do so.[3]

Furthermore, since it is generally assumed that a person
should be accepted as what he claims to be, should be taken
at face value and given the benefit of the doubt, advanta-
geous definitions of any situations based upon technical
performance are more difficult to secure than those based
upon dramaturgy, upon impression management. It is easier
to be what you say you are than what you do. In this connection, people seem to be more concerned with the right to
give a performance than with the performance itself. Even
though the performance is outstanding, if the person did not
have the right to perform, he is severely criticized, perhaps

---

in ch. iv. In Goffman's dramaturgical terms, these symbols act as scenery
and help make the performance impressive.

[2] Goffman: op. cit., pp. 46, 58-66. Performers usually foster this
impression.

[3] Popular and journalistic interpretations of affairs are consistently
based upon the identification of right and ability, resulting in a strange,
charismatic, personalized interpretation of events as outcomes of high-
level personal interactions. The assumed sacred compatibility between
the man and the role acts as a legitimization of any *de facto* power or
wealth. "He must be a very able man because he gets all that money,"
or "He must be the smartest man there because he is the boss." Thus,
power and wealth are held to be their own justification. We do not
need to go beyond their possession. Perhaps this kind of circularity was
an ideological necessity at the time the middle class was struggling for
power with feudalism. It has always created uncomfortable uncertain-
ties in connection with out-and-out criminally obtained wealth and
power. It also encourages phantasies and wishful thinking about lucky
windfalls ("when my ship comes in"), perhaps encourages crime, and
certainly encourages give-away shows on TV.

even jailed as an impostor.[4] Conversely, even though the performance is of low quality, the right to give it will protect it from criticism. Here again the hierarchical role is fortunately situated, insofar as inability to perform will be masked by the undoubted right to do so. The same is true of well-established specialist roles, like that of the doctor, of the lawyer, or of the engineer.

4. The Management Troupe

Successful performances demand the loyalty of the performers, the solidarity of the performing team. Since the control of impressions requires the careful withholding and editing of information imparted to the audience, it is imperative that all members of the team be trustworthy, that they be discreet with regard to the facts relevant to the performance. This solidarity can be promoted by making the audience a "race apart," and particularly by demeaning the audience, by conceiving of it as being composed of people of lesser stature.[5] Demeaning the audience also protects the performers from their own deceit, both emotionally and morally—the deceit that the performers, or occupants of hierarchical roles, are superior, more dependable, more industrious, more loyal, and therefore more important to the organization.[6] The gen-

[4] Goffman: op. cit., p. 59. He says the better the impostor's performance, the more we feel threatened because the situation challenges the assumed sacred relation between the man and the role.

[5] Note the reported hidden ridicule of Chinese prison guards and interrogators by American prisoners in the Korean War. E. H. Schein: "The Chinese Indoctrination Program for Prisoners of War," *Psychiatry*, Vol. XIX (1956), pp. 149-72.

[6] See Goffman: op. cit., pp. 214-15. When the performers are subordinate to the audience, as employees are in the performances they must present to superiors, derogation of the audience serves the additional purpose of recapturing the performers' self-respect. "But secret derogation seems to be much more common than secret praise, perhaps because such derogation serves to maintain the solidarity of the team, demonstrating mutual regard at the expense of those absent and compensating, perhaps, for the loss of self-respect that may occur when the audience must be accorded accommodative face-to-face treatment."

eral dramaturgical framework provided by the status system serves the purpose of dehumanizing the audience of subordinates. They are mere lower-status employees, "subordinates," childlike creatures both unskilled and undependable, requiring "close supervision." The derogation of specialist roles serves the same purpose.

The loyalty of the performing team is assured by practicing rotation to avoid a sympathetic attachment to the audience. If a superior becomes too closely identified with his subordinates, he is regarded as "useless" to the management and must be removed or transferred.

More important than rotation in assuring the solidarity of the team is the careful selection of persons to be admitted to the team. Careful selection not only insures loyalty, but it also guarantees ability to perform the required routine. Furthermore, each member of the team is part of the staging props, background, or scenery against which the performance must be presented. Since much of the information conveyed to the audience is by visible rather than verbal symbols, the appearances and mannerisms of the performers cannot be overlooked.

Consequently, hierarchical roles cannot be filled by reference to technical qualifications alone. The real check is not a merit examination but a suitability interview, and for a person being considered for promotion, long and close observation by a superior. Various physical features have doomed persons to lower-level positions.[7] Physical appearance, dress, mannerisms, office behavior—all are important. Impressions fostered at work are probably as important as accomplishment. The person to be absorbed into the team

---

(Ibid., p. 171.) The manipulative approach fails to realize that the subordinate's behavior is also a performance, that subordinates control managerial impressions. Because of this interrelation, direct knowledge of employee morale or regard for management can rarely be obtained. Instead, inferences must be drawn from various indices, such as absenteeism, turnover, output, etc. Inferences drawn from output are particularly liable to be in error. See Whyte: op. cit., pp. 63-4; and James G. March and Herbert A. Simon: *Organizations* (New York: John Wiley & Sons, Inc.; 1958), pp. 47-8.

[7] See pp. 142-3 ft. nt. 9, above.

must have shown his ability to create the impressions of busyness, loyalty, "sound judgment," etc.

It is especially important in the selection process to determine the discretion of the person to be admitted to the team. He must have no black spots on his record; and a good record is most easily achieved by "going along with the gang," by avoiding risky innovations or ideas. He must not appear too intellectual, nor too technically skilled; and he must at least appear to place the good of the team above his profession.[8]

Higher positions are frequently filled by the sponsorship system. Promising youngsters who appear to be "our kind" are carefully prepared for the later assumption of high managerial positions.[9] Persons selected for the team must possess "dramaturgical discipline."[1] They must be able to control their emotions, to be "on top" of their performance, and to control their hostilities. Control of face, voice, and

[8] It has often been reported that professional and technical specialists are vaguely distrusted by managements. It is feared, probably with good reason, that they might not go "all the way down the line" for the organization, especially if its demands conflicted with their professional code of conduct. See Gouldner: op. cit., pp. 225-7; Whyte: op. cit., pp. 164, 182; and Mills: op. cit., pp. 138-46. In an illustration of what he means by "responsibility," Barnard indicated he expects the loyal employee to put the good of the organization ahead of even the lives of family members. *The Functions of the Executive* (Cambridge: Harvard University Press; 1947), p. 269.

[9] The preference for middle- and upper-class individuals is understandable as a device for protecting the backstage. Despite the "open class myth," itself a legitimating ideology, the upper hierarchy is largely reserved for middle- and upper-class persons. Of the very top business executives in this country in 1951, 57 percent were the sons of businessmen, 14 percent the sons of professional people, 15 percent the sons of farmers, and only 12 percent the sons of wage earners; C. Wright Mills: op. cit., pp. 127-8. Of the 1952 executives under 50, only 2½ percent had wage-earner origins, "The Nine Hundred," *Fortune* (November 1952), pp. 132 ff. The social origins of top government executives are predominantly middle class. Reinhard Bendix: "Who are the Government Bureaucrats?," in Gouldner, ed.: op. cit., pp. 330-41.

[1] Goffman: op. cit., pp. 216-18. "Perhaps the focus of dramaturgical discipline is to be found in the management of one's face and voice." Ibid., p. 217.

gesture is central here.[2] Without dramaturgical discipline, the performer might make an improper disclosure or extend to the audience the status of team members.

Behavior away from work is no less important than behavior at work. An embarrassing disclosure in only one aspect of a person's role, in one routine among many, is likely to discredit the many other areas of activity in which he has nothing to conceal.[3] His church, his clubs, the location of his home, his children's school, his wife, his home life, all are matters which might discredit the desired impression as an upper-hierarchical-role occupant. And since the discrediting of one performer on the team might discredit the whole team's performance, all of these private matters become relevant in choosing a person for admission to the team. Undoubtedly, this consideration is an important reason for the deplored invasion of private life by modern organizations.

5. *Subordinate Dramaturgy*

Although we have stressed the management of impressions by superiors, subordinates must also engage in this kind of behavior. In general, subordinates must create the impression that they are awed by their superiors, that the latters' performance has gone off well. This is simply a reflection of

---

[2] "In my judgment, confirmed by others whose opinion I respect, it is as a general rule exceedingly bad practice for one in a superior position to swear at or in the presence of those of subordinate or inferior status . . . I have known very few men who could do it without adverse reactions on their influence. I suppose the reason is that whatever lowers the dignity of a superior position makes it more difficult to accept difference of position." Chester Barnard: *Organization and Management* (Cambridge: Harvard University Press; 1949), pp. 73-4; quoted in Goffman: op. cit., p. 199. Actually, swearing in this situation is inconsistent with the lofty impression projected by the higher-status person.

[3] Goffman: op. cit., pp. 64-5. In this respect, note the destruction of Sherman Adams's image presented to the world by the minor and rather silly disclosures in regard to Bernard Goldfine.

their need to please the boss.[4] Subordinates must create the impression that they *need* to be told what to do; that they *need* to be told how to do it; and, in general, that they could not get along without the boss. Since the superior is presented as the initiating and creative force, subordinates must convey the impression that all of their ideas and actions are *his* actions. Since the superior is presented as the busiest and most important person, subordinates must create the impression that they understand that he has little time to deal with them and their relatively unimportant problems. Many subordinates, therefore, attempt communication with the boss infrequently and briefly. Interviews, telephone conversations, and memos may be few and brief.[5] Since the superior is presented as the person with the greatest intellectual and moral qualities, subordinates must create the impression that they feel awed and humble in his presence. As in the case with superordinate impression management, the status system aids subordinate impression management by keeping the audience and performers segregated and by protecting the backstage, with all of its performance-discrediting information. It is backstage that one finds out what subordinates really think about their superiors.

[4] Harold Leavitt says any job is actually two jobs. "One is to carry out the assignment, to get the job done; the other . . . job is to please the superior." *Managerial Psychology* (Chicago: University of Chicago Press; 1958), p. 264.

[5] There is also the status-hungry "climber" who attempts a great deal of communication with superiors as a device for enhancing his status *vis-à-vis* his peers. One suspects that this kind of "pushy" behavior is not usually rewarded by co-optation into the "management team." See Robert K. Merton: "Continuities in the Theory of Reference Groups and Social Structure," in *Social Theory and Social Structure*, rev. ed. (Glencoe, Illinois: The Free Press; 1957).

CHAPTER 8

Bureaupathology

♯♯

1. *Bureaupathic Behavior*

DEPENDENCE upon specialization imparts to modern organizations certain qualities which we discussed in chapter two. Among these are routinization, strong attachment to subgoals, impersonality, categorization, resistance to change, etc. The individual must adjust to these qualities because they cannot be eliminated from bureaucratic organization. In our society there are many people who have been unable to make this adjustment and who therefore find modern organization a constant source of frustration. They suffer from the social disease of "bureausis." In the last part of this chapter we shall try to diagnose this disease.

Personal behavior patterns are frequently encountered which exaggerate the characteristic qualities of bureaucratic organization. Within bureaucracy we often find excessive aloofness, ritualistic attachment to routines and procedures, and resistance to change; and associated with these behavior patterns is a petty insistence upon rights of authority and status. From the standpoint of organizational goal ac complishment, these personal behavior patterns are patholog- ical because they do not advance organizational goals. They reflect the personal needs of individuals. To the extent that criticism of modern bureaucracy is not "bureautic," it is directed at these self-serving personal behavior patterns. Responsible criticism of bureaucratic pathology does not constitute a nostalgic longing to go back to a simpler era, but is an attempt to find the causes of pathological behavior with the hope of eliminating it. When people use the term "bureau- cratic" in a critical sense, they are frequently referring to these personally oriented behavior patterns. Because the term is also used in a descriptive, noncritical sense, as Weber used it and as it has been used throughout this book, we shall avoid this critical use of the term and use in its stead a word which clearly denotes the pathological. We shall call these behaviors "bureaupathic."

The appropriation of major aspects of bureaucratic or- ganization as means for the satisfaction of personal needs is pathological. It is a form of behavior which is functional for less than the system as a whole, including in this connection the clientele as part of the system. It involves a shifting in the costs[1] of the system by those with more authority to those with less, be they subordinates or clientele. It is a kind of behavior possible to those in the organization who have the best opportunity to use the organization to satisfy per- sonal needs, namely, those in authority positions. It can only be exercised "downward." It cannot be exercised by clientele over authoritative officials, and it cannot be exer-

[1] The obligation to accept another's decision may have a number of negative aspects, or *costs*. First is the dislike of subordination itself. Furthermore, the decision may not accord with one's moral beliefs, or it may conflict with one's self-interest. It may not appeal to one's rea- son and is likely in any case to require some change in habits. There- fore, the possible costs involved in being a subordinate or a regulated client are subordination costs, moral costs, self-interest costs, rationality costs, and inertial costs. See Herbert A. Simon, Donald W. Smithburg, and Victor A. Thompson: *Public Administration* (New York: Alfred A. Knopf; 1959), ch. xxi.

cised by subordinates over superiors. It is, in short, a phenomenon of the system of authority, both hierarchical and nonhierarchical.[2]

2. *Insecurity and the Need to Control*

This pathological behavior starts with a need on the part of the person in an authority position to control those subordinate to himself. To "control" means to have subordinate behavior correspond as closely as possible with one set of preconceived standards. While the need to control arises in large part from personal insecurity in the superior, it has conceptual sources as well, which we shall briefly state.

In the United States, we have still the ghost of the absolute king in the guise of the theory of sovereignty. Sovereignty theory supports the monistic conception of bureaucratic organization, with its associated institution of hierarchy. The superior has the right, by delegation ultimately from the absolute sovereign, to obtain a unique outcome; and he has the duty, or the responsibility to his superior, to obtain it. In profit organizations, it is held that there is only one outcome which will satisfy profit maximization under the specific conditions of the market. It is also held that the duty to seek this outcome is an overriding one because only in this way can the welfare of all be best promoted, even though in individual instances it may not seem so. In the

[2] Writers on bureaucracy like Merton, Selznick, Gouldner and others use essentially the same concept of "bureaucratic," although, except by Gouldner, the distinction between the descriptive and critical sense of the term is never made clear. In general, they start with a need of some authority figure for control, followed by behavior which creates conditions exaggerating the need for control, etc., in a vicious circle. On this point see James G. March and Herbert A. Simon: *Organizations* (New York: John Wiley & Sons, Inc.; 1958), pp. 36-46; and Chris Argyris: "The Individual and Organization: Some Problems of Mutual Adjustment," *Admin. Sci. Q.*, Vol. II (1957), pp. 1-22, and "Understanding Human Behavior in Organizations: One Viewpoint," in Mason Haire, ed.: *Modern Organization Theory* (New York: John Wiley & Sons, Inc.; 1959).

monocratic society of Russia, only one outcome can be tolerated because only one is consistent with the laws of history; only one is possible. (Why it is necessary to seek bureaucratic control in the face of this historical determinism has never been satisfactorily explained so far as we know.)

Although these conceptual sources for the need to control exist, they are hardly compelling. Much more important in explaining the authoritative need to control is personal insecurity.[3] Here we may well recap these sources of personal insecurity and anxiety in modern bureaucratic organization.

Hierarchical structure with its monopoly of "success" is a potent source of anxiety. The person in a superordinate position has a near final control over the satisfaction of subordinates' needs, their personal goals.[4] While at the bottom of the hierarchy the standards which must be met are frequently made explicit and objectively measurable, managerial personnel have generally resisted a like invasion of their own superordinate rights.[5] As we have said before, the objectivity of performance standards decreases as one mounts the hierarchy until at some point they become largely subjective. At the same time, we would expect an increasing concentration of success-hungry people in the upper reaches of the hierarchy. Strong status needs and strong doubts as to what will please the person who can satisfy those needs can only result in anxiety and, for many, in

[3] Although the conceptual basis for the need to control is more thoroughly worked out in Russia, it has been observed that the attempt by Russian top management to concentrate power and control in its own hands results from insecurity generated by pressure from above. See Reinhard Bendix: *Work and Authority in Industry* (New York: John Wiley & Sons, Inc.; 1956), ch. vi.

[4] For a theory of individual accommodation to the organization based on hierarchically generated anxiety, see Robert V. Presthus: "Toward a Theory of Organizational Behavior," *Admin. Sci. Q.*, Vol. III, No. 1 (June 1958), pp. 48 ff. See also Peter Blau: *The Dynamics of Bureaucracy* (Chicago: University of Chicago Press; 1955), p. 173.

[5] This resistance was apparently the basis of the managerial opposition to Taylorism and Scientific Management generally. See Bendix: op. cit. pp. 274-81.

"automaton conformity" [6] to the wishes of the boss. Hierarchical anxiety is much like Calvinism in that it generates painful doubt as to who is chosen. Like Calvinism, these doubts can be reduced, not only by automaton conformity but by excessive activity and the appearance of extreme busyness.[7]

Anxiety is also associated with insecurity of function. To occupy a position not fully accepted by significant others in the organization tends to make one isolated, a minority in a hostile world. This kind of insecurity may result from a new specialty not yet fully accredited and accepted; or it may result from the authoritative assignment of jurisdiction (the delegation of nonhierarchical authority) in defiance of the needs of specialization.

Finally, the source of insecurity which is becoming the most significant in modern organizations is the growing gap between the rights of authority (to review, to veto, to affirm) and the specialized ability or skill required to solve most organizational problems. The intellectual, problem-solving, content of executive positions is being increasingly diverted to specialists, leaving hierarchical rights (and duties) as the principal components of executive posts.[8] Persons in

[6] See Erich Fromm: *Escape From Freedom* (New York: Holt, Rinehart and Winston, Inc.; 1941), p. 185. See also Clara Thompson: *Psychoanalysis: Evolution and Development* (New York: Thomas Nelson & Sons; 1950), p. 208. See also Fromm: *Man for Himself: An Inquiry into the Psychology of Ethics* (New York: Holt, Rinehart and Winston, Inc.; 1947), p. 72. Of 75 middle-management people questioned by Harold Leavitt, most thought that conformance to the wishes of the boss was the principal criterion for evaluating subordinates. Harold J. Leavitt: *Managerial Psychology* (Chicago: University of Chicago Press; 1958), p. 288.

[7] See Rollo May: *The Meaning of Anxiety* (New York: The Ronald Press Company; 1950), p. 172.

[8] For a discussion of this process in industrial management, see Bendix: op. cit., pp. 226 ff. His discussion is based on a work by Ernest Dale: *Planning and Developing the Company Organization Structure* (New York: American Management Association, Inc.; 1952), Research Report No. 20. Advancing specialization in the problem-solving aspect of organizations is further reflected in these figures from Bendix: op. cit., pp. 211 ff. Between 1899 and 1947 the proportion of administrative

hierarchical positions are therefore increasingly dependent upon subordinate and nonsubordinate specialists for the achievement of organizational (or unit) goals. The superior tends to be caught between the two horns of a dilemma. He must satisfy the nonexplicit and nonoperational demands of a superior through the agency of specialized subordinates and nonsubordinates whose skills he only dimly understands.[9] And yet, to be counted a success he must accept this dilemma and live with its increasing viciousness throughout his life. He must live with increasing insecurity and anxiety.[1] Although a particular person may have great maturity and general psychological security, an insecure superior at any point in the hierarchy above him can, and probably will, generate pressures which must inevitably be passed down the line, creating insecurity and tensions all the way to the bottom.[2] Given a person's hierarchical relationship with his superior, he is always subject to blame for outcomes which he could control only remotely, if at all.

---

to production workers in American industry increased from 7.7 percent to 21.6 percent. From 1910 to 1940 the work force in America increased by 49 percent. Entrepreneurs increased by 17 percent; manual workers, by 49 percent; and salaried employees, by 127 percent. Bendix sees bureaucratization in industry as the continuing subdivision of the functions of the early owner-manager.

[9] Of course, the extent of the dilemma varies with position in the hierarchy and with the extent to which complex specialties are required by the particular organization. The ongoing process of specialization will move the dilemma down the hierarchy and to more and more organizations.

[1] Middle-management executives interviewed by William H. Whyte referred to their lives as "treadmills" or "rat races," thereby expressing the tensions generated by this dilemma. *The Organization Man* (Garden City, New York: Doubleday & Company, Inc.; 1953), p. 176.

[2] William Caudill has shown that tensions starting at the very top of a mental hospital were easily communicated all the way down to the patients, creating symptoms in them that were generated entirely within the hospital. *The Psychiatric Hospital as a Small Society* (Cambridge: Harvard University Press; 1958).

3. *The Bureaupathic Reaction*

Insecurity gives rise to personal (nonorganizational) needs which may be generalized in the need for control. This need often results in behavior which appears irrational from the standpoint of the organization's goals because it does not advance them; it advances only personal goals and satisfies only personal needs. In so doing, it creates conditions which do not eliminate the need for control but rather enhance it.[3]

Alvin W. Gouldner studied the succession to the position of plant manager by a man from outside the plant.[4] This man was obligated to upper management and felt duty-bound to realize its efficiency and production values. He started out, therefore, with heavy pressure from above. Coming from outside, he did not understand the informal

---

[3] March and Simon (op. cit.) criticize some of the sociological treatments of bureaupathic behavior because they feel that these theories do not explain why functional learning on the part of authority figures does not take place. It will be recalled that these theories posit a need for control, followed by behaviors which create conditions which exaggerate the need for control. If this behavior is conceived as organization problem solving, there is indeed a problem of functional learning involved. However, bureaupathic behavior is functional in personal rather than organizational terms. It must be admitted that most of these sociological treatments do not clearly distinguish beween personal and organizational goals—between bureaupathic and bureaucratic behavior. The "dysfunctional learning" involved is failure to learn that employees cannot very effectively be treated according to the machine model. However, this learning can be considered dysfunctional only by applying the machine model to management. If management operated like a rational machine, it would learn that employees are not machines. The basic methodological flaw of the "management" approach is that it assumes that persons described by the term "management" behave according to sociopsychological laws different from those governing the behavior of others—that the manager is an independent variable in the organization.

[4] The following discussion of succession is taken from his *Patterns of Industrial Bureaucracy* (Glencoe, Illinois: The Free Press; 1954), Part Two.

system prevailing in the plant and was unable to use it. As his insecurity and anxiety mounted, he turned more and more to the formal system of rules, defined competencies, impersonality, and close supervision. He met resistance and felt his position between the horns of the dilemma, between those above and those below, increasingly insecure. He reacted with increased aloofness and formality. He exaggerated the characteristics of bureaucratic organization. He became bureaupathic.

The example illustrates the circularity in the bureaupathic reaction. Since the manager's behavior was so strongly influenced by his personal needs to reduce his own anxiety, the employees' responses deviated more and more from organizational needs, thereby increasing the manager's anxiety and completing the circle. The mechanisms underlying this process are not difficult to understand. Control standards encourage minimal participation.[5] They encourage employees to meet the standards and no more. Furthermore, meeting the control devices tends to become the aim of the subordinates because that is how they manage their own insecurities and avoid sanctions. For example, if agents are rated on the number of violations they uncover, cases of compliance are not likely to give them great joy.[6] Strict control from above encourages employees to "go by the book," to avoid innovations and chances of errors which put black marks on the record. It encourages the accumulation of records to prove compliance, resulting in *paperasserie*, as the French call it.[7] It encourages decision by precedent, and unwillingness to exercise initiative or take a chance. It encourages employees to wait for orders and do only what they are told. It is not hard to understand, therefore, why the superior may come to feel that he must apply more control. If he is also subject to strict bureaupathic control from above, this situation is likely to contribute to ulcers, if not, indeed, to complete breakdown.

[5] Ibid., pp. 174-6.
[6] See Blau: op. cit., p. 192.
[7] Walter Rice Sharp: *The French Civil Service: Bureaucracy in Transition* (New York: The Macmillan Co.; 1931), pp. 446-50.

4. *The Drift to Quantitative Compliance*

An exaggerated dependence upon regulations and quantitative standards is likely to stem from a supervisor's personal insecurity in the parentlike role of the boss. It has been observed that women supervisors are more likely to insist upon strict compliance with all organizational rules and regulations than are men. The bureaupathic tendency of women has been attributed to their greater insecurity in the superordinate role because the general role of women in our society is somewhat subordinate.[8] A battery of regulations makes it unnecessary for the superior to give the detailed face-to-face order very often. Everybody, including the supervisor, is simply carrying out instructions imposed from above. If they are unpleasant instructions, it is not the supervisor's fault. For much the same reason, an insecure superior will probably appreciate a large number of quantitative control standards because his ratings of his subordinates then appear to be inevitable results of the performances of the subordinates, not merely the personal judgments of the superior. The anger and aggressions of the subordinates can then be displaced to the impersonal "system," and the superior can continue to get their indispensable co-operation upon which his own "success" depends.[9] Furthermore, disparities of power are hidden by the rules, and if punishment is meted out, it comes from the rules, not from the superior. In all of these ways, the rules and regulations make the parentlike role less uncomfortable for insecure people.[1]

[8] See Arnold W. Green and Eleanor Melnick: "What Has Happened to the Feminist Movement," Alvin W. Gouldner, ed.: *Studies in Leadership: Leadership and Democratic Action* (New York: Harper & Brothers; 1950), pp. 277-302.

[9] See Blau: op. cit., pp. 175-6.

[1] Gouldner: *Patterns of Industrial Bureaucracy*, ch. ix. On the relationship between ritualistic compliance with regulations and personal insecurity, see Rose Laub Coser: "Authority and Decision Making in a Hospital: A Comparative Analysis," *Am. Sociol. Rev.* (February 1958). See also Reinhard Bendix: *Higher Civil Servants in American*

Only the observable and measurable aspects of behavior can be controlled. These aspects are often the most trivial and unimportant from the standpoint of the long-range success of the organization. Where the need to control exists, therefore, it often manifests itself in procedures, reports, and clearances governing trivia, while at the same time very important matters are left to discretion because controlling them is not feasible. The need to control is sufficiently widespread to have given sometimes a petty and ludicrous quality to modern organization. We venture to predict that if one looks hard enough in any modern organization, he will find instructions just as ridiculous as those of the military on how to wash a dog, pick a flower, or use a fork.[2] Since the controls can successfully be applied only to the observable and measurable aspects of a job, and since the employee must concentrate on satisfying the control standards in order to reduce his own personal insecurities, his emphasis shifts from the more important, qualitative aspects of the job to the less important, quantitative aspects. In an employment office, for example, the goal shifted from good placement, in the beginning, to the highest possible number of people put to work. Interviewers felt constrained to use whatever sanctions they had to induce a client to take a job, whether he wanted it and was suited to it or not.[3]

5. *Exaggerated Aloofness*

Organizational relationships are by nature less warm and personal than the relations of friendship. It is only when this

---

Society (Boulder, Colorado: University of Colorado Press; 1949), pp. 14-19, 112-22.

[2] There is another source of extreme, detailed controls in modern organizations, one which can be dealt with rationally. Units are frequently established whose goals are defined *entirely* in terms of writing instructions. Since they have nothing assigned to them except to write instructions, in time they can be expected to "cover" everything—even as a monkey, if given enough time on the typewriter, would eventually type out the complete works of Shakespeare. Involved in this situation is goal factoring, not bureaupathic behavior.

[3] Blau: op. cit., p. 96.

impersonality is exaggerated to cold aloofness and apparent disinterest that we can with any fairness call it pathological. As with other kinds of bureaupathic behavior, exaggerated aloofness can usually be attributed to personal insecurity.

A cold aloofness protects an insecure superior from commitments to his subordinates which he fears will be inconsistent with demands upon him from above. It makes it easier for him to mete out punishment or to perform other aspects of his hierarchical role, such as rating his subordinates. It protects him from the aggressions of his subordinates by maintaining a psychic distance between him and them. In extreme cases it can come close to a complete breakdown of communication between the superior and his subordinates.

The same considerations apply to relations between officials and clients. A certain impersonality is necessary both to protect the goals of the organization and to secure objective and therefore effective service to the client. This impersonality may be exaggerated into a cold disinterest by an insecure official. When officials are caught between demands or "rights" of clients and tight administrative controls from above, dissociation from the clients and disinterest in their problems may seem to be the only way out of the dilemma. Client hostility, generated by what appears to be official emphasis on the wrong goals, creates tension. Inconsiderate treatment of the clients may become a device for reducing tensions and maintaining the cohesion of the officials. Blau has shown how such a situation leads to backstage demeaning of clients which, by putting psychic distance between the officials and the clients, protects the officials. Officials then tend to seek satisfactions from the abstract values of the enterprise rather than from the concrete values of personal service to a client.[4]

Within the organization, technically unnecessary interdependence creates insecurity of function. As we have seen in previous chapters, authority is sometimes delegated for

[4] Ibid., pp. 91-5. See also Erving Goffman: *The Presentation of Self in Everyday Life* (Garden City, New York: Doubleday & Company, Inc.; 1959), p. 177.

political rather than technical reasons, to meet personal rather than organizational needs. Because the resulting relationship is not accepted and is constantly under attack, the person with the delegated authority lives in insecurity. Here, also, patterns of cold and imperious aloofness are often observed, and abstract values rather than personal service become goals. Officials exercising such disputed, delegated authority frequently demean their clients as narrow-minded, if not stupid. Procedures to govern the relationship are elaborated and, because they stabilize the relationship, such procedures acquire an exaggerated value for these officials.

6. Resistance to Change

Bureaucratic organizations have to administer change carefully, as we pointed out in chapter two. Perhaps most people resist change just for the sake of change. The burden of proof is on the side of those advocating change. However, resistance to change may also be exaggerated by insecure officials; it may become bureaupathic. In an organizational context dominated by the need to control, innovation is dangerous because, by definition, it is not controlled behavior. It creates risks of errors and therefore of sanctions. To encourage innovation, an insecure superior would have to extend the initiative to subordinates and thereby lose control. Furthermore, in an insecure, competitive group situation, innovation threatens the security of all members of the group and for this reason tends to be suppressed by informal group action, as well as by the insecure superior. Innovation is facilitated by a secure, noncompetitive group administrative effort dominated by a professional outlook. Since this kind of situation is thought to be rare in modern bureaucracy, some people might regard excessive resistance to change as an inherent feature of bureaucratic organization, rather than as a form of bureaupathology. We feel, however, that excessive bureaucratic inertia is much less widespread than is supposed.[5] In an era of ever more rapid change, it

[5] In a state employment office and a federal enforcement agency,

seems unlikely that man has evolved a kind of organization which is particularly resistive to innovation. The traditionalistic organization was the kind most resistive, and in many places it had to be blasted off the scene by revolutionary action. The bureaucratic form replaced it, partly because it was able to accommodate to a changing world.

There is another source of resistance to change which is not bureaupathic and which is therefore subject to rational corrective procedures. The communication pattern determines who gets feed-back information. A particular official may never get intimate knowledge of the results of his own actions. Consequently, he may feel no need for a change which others who do have this knowledge think should be made. Bringing the "offending" official into direct communication with respondents might cure in a hurry this particular case of resistance to change.

7. Insistence on the Rights of Office

The bureaupathic official usually exaggerates the official, nontechnical aspects of relationships and suppresses the technical and the informal. He stresses rights, not abilities. Since his behavior stems from insecurity, he may be expected to insist on petty rights and prerogatives, on protocol, on procedure—in short, on those things least likely to affect directly the goal accomplishment of the organization. For example, a rather functionless reviewing officer will often insist most violently on his right of review and scream like an injured animal if he is by-passed. He will often insist on petty changes, such as minor changes in the wording of a

Blau found little evidence of resistance to change. The cases he did find were based upon the fear of a superior and fear of the loss of security in relations with subordinates or clients. (Op. cit., pp. 184-9.) He found that new employees and less competent employees were more resistive to change than others. (Ibid., p. 197.) He found also that ritualistic compliance with rules and regulations stemmed from personal insecurity in important relationships at work. (Ibid., p. 188.) Secure officials welcomed change because it made their work interesting by providing new challenges.

document. If he has a counterpart at a higher organizational level, he will probably insist on exclusive contact with that higher clearance point. By controlling this particular communication channel he protects his authority and influence, even perhaps enhancing them somewhat by being the sole interpreter of the higher-clearance-point's requirements.[6] In like fashion and for the same reasons, an insecure superior can be expected to exert his right to the monopoly of outgoing and incoming communication. Everything must go through "formal channels." In this way he can hide his weakness and suppress information which might reveal his insecurity. He also hopes to maintain his influence and authority by suppressing the influence of external specialists, the "staff." One of the great difficulties of modern organization arises from the inescapable fact that specialist communication must break through such blockades.

Insistence upon the full rights of the superordinate role is what is meant by "close supervision." It seems to be related to doubts about the loyalty or ability of subordinates, combined with pressure from above.[7] Close supervision can be regarded as bureaupathic under conditions where the right to act and the ability to do so have become separated because of the advance of specialization. However, where the position has a great deal of technical content so that subordinates are technically dependent upon their supervisor, as in a railroad maintenance section, close supervision may be tolerated and even demanded by subordinates. It may be a necessary means to the organization's goal. The right to supervise closely gets further legitimation from the technical ability to do so.[8]

[6] See Victor A. Thompson: *The Regulatory Process in OPA Rationing* (New York: King's Crown Press; 1950), pp. 298-303.

[7] In addition to other references cited throughout this chapter, see Walter L. Dorn: "The Prussian Bureaucracy in the 18th Century," *Polit. Sci. Rev.*, Vol. XLVI (September 1931). See also Alexander Barmine: *One Who Survived* (New York: G. P. Putnam's Sons; 1945); and "The Stewardship of Sewell Avery," *Fortune*, Vol. XXXIII (May 1946).

[8] See D. Katy, N. Maccoby, G. Gurin, and L. G. Floor: *Productivity, Supervision and Morale among Railroad Workers* (Ann Arbor:

8. Bureaupathology and Organization Structure

Institutions are staffed by persons, and so personality is always an element in institutional behavior. It will account for differences of degree and minor variations in form. For the major outlines of institutional behavior, however, we must seek the causes in the institutions themselves. Bureaupathic behavior is caused by the structures and conditions within our bureaucratic organizations. To say this is not to deny the reinforcing impact of personality. Some people are undoubtedly more inclined than others to be aloof, to get enmeshed in details, to be officious, to be excessively cautious, to be insensitive to others, to be insecure. What we do deny is that there is a bureaupathic personality type, or that observed cases of bureaupathic behavior will always, or even usually, be associated with one type of person.[9] Any person, regardless of personality type, may behave in some or all of the ways we have just described under the appropriate conditions, and these conditions occur very frequently in the modern bureaucratic organization.

It has been argued that a kind of rigidity grows out of prolonged role enactment, and that bureaucrats, over a period of time, become insensitive to the needs of clients.[1] We

---

Survey Research Center, University of Michigan; 1951). See also A. W. Halpin: "The Leadership Behavior and Combat Performance of Airplane Commanders," *J. Abnorm. and Soc. Psychol.*, Vol. XLIX (1954), pp. 19-22.

[9] For example, attempts have been made to show that "compulsive neurotics" predominate in bureaucracy. See Otto Sperling: "Psychoanalytic Aspects of Bureaucracy," *Psychoan. Q.*, Vol. XIX (1950), pp. 88-100.

[1] Theodore R. Sarbin: "Role Theory," in Gardner Lindzey, ed.: *Handbook of Social Psychology* (Reading, Massachusetts: Addison-Wesley Publishing Company, Inc.; 1954), Vol. I, pp. 223-58. Sarbin points out that this proposition is only an hypothesis, and one would have to find these qualities of rigidity and impersonality in non-occupational behavior as well in order to demonstrate it. We might point out that one would also have to show that these qualities were not present at the beginning of the period of "prolonged role enact-

have shown that a certain impersonal treatment is inherent in bureaucratic structure. The charge of insensitivity may therefore be a bureautic reaction. One must not forget that clients are notoriously insensitive to the needs of bureaucrats. The question is, when does bureaucratic insensitivity become pathological? In many bureaucratic organizations, relations with clients are warm and cordial, as for example, between the postman and the householder.

Although prolonged role enactment undoubtedly has a profound effect on a person,[2] what is the "bureaucratic role?" People move around quite freely in bureaucracies. They perform various roles. We do not think it makes sense to speak of the "bureaucratic role." We have emphasized specialist roles and hierarchical roles. In the hierarchy, people go from position to position as they advance. Specialists often move from organization to organization. The truly prolonged role is the entrepreneurial professional role, such as the physician. It seems doubtful that physicians, as a group, are "insensitive to the needs of clients."

Although there is no "bureaucratic role," there is bureaucratic structure. It is obvious that some people are able to achieve personal goals within this structure more easily and comfortably than others. These people have been called bureaucratic types; but they are not necessarily bureaupathic. In fact, it may be that the person who moves most

---

ment." Sarbin relies somewhat on Robert K. Merton's well-known essay, "Bureaucratic Structure and Personality," in *Social Theory and Social Structure*, rev. ed. (Glencoe, Illinois: The Free Press; 1957). However, Merton does not seem to be talking about the interaction of self and role. Generally, he is explaining "bureaucratic" behavior by reference to bureaucratic structure (graded careers, seniority, *esprit de corps*, the appropriateness of secondary, i.e., impersonal, relations, etc.). He also suggests that the ideal patterns of bureaucratic behavior become exaggerated by being affectively backed, as we have argued. However, he does not explain the origin of this affect ("sentiments") to our satisfaction. We have argued that it comes from personal insecurity in an authority position. Merton does not distinguish between the descriptive and critical uses of the term "bureaucratic."

[2] See Willard Waller: *The Sociology of Teaching* (New York: John Wiley & Sons, Inc.; 1932).

easily within the bureaucratic structure is the one who can hide his insecurity, his "inner rumblings," as Whyte puts it. His insecurity may express itself internally as ulcers but not externally as bureaupathic behavior.

Bureaupathic behavior is one result of the growing insecurity of authority in modern organizations. This insecurity exists because nonhierarchical authority is so frequently delegated without regard to the ability to exercise it; such is the practice of politics.[3] More important, however, is the fact that the culturally defined institution of hierarchy, with its rather extreme claim of rights, is increasingly uncomfortable with advancing specialization. Hierarchical rights change slowly; specialization, the result of technology, changes with increasing speed. The situation is unstable. The legitimacy of organizational authority is in danger. Bureaupathic behavior is one result of this situation.

9. *Bureaupathology and Routinization*

The bureaupathic response to insecurity is facilitated by the routinization of organizational problem solving. When the development of appropriate routines is the dominant imperative, when technical problems must be solved, the emphasis must be on abilities rather than rights.[4] Charismatic

---

[3] In organizational terms, politics means those activities concerned with the delegation of authority on bases other than a generally recognized ability to exercise it. It involves some kind of exchange between the person desiring the authority and the authority figure who has it to give. It is made possible by the fact that authority may be delegated. Since the specialist content of executive positions is increasingly attenuated as one mounts the hierarchy, so that ability criteria become less and less relevant, placement in these positions becomes more and more a political phenomenon, a matter of "office politics"; the incumbents are "political types." See Harold Lasswell: *Politics: Who Gets What, When, How* (New York: McGraw-Hill Book Co.; 1936).

[4] Studies of decision-making groups in business and government show that the groups prefer strict and formal performances by the conference leader when the subject matter is trivial but not when the subject is important. L. Berkowitz: "Sharing Leadership in Small,

patterns predominate. These facts are illustrated by wartime experience.

When World War II broke out, a large regulatory structure had to be quickly created. People with many types of skill, from many walks of life, and with many different statuses were quickly assembled in Washington. A whole host of brand new problems was given to them. In those early days, emphasis was on technical problem solving. Anyone who could come up with an idea on how to proceed "got ahead." Bureaupathic patterns were almost nonexistent. The emphasis was on what one could do, not on rights and prerogatives. People became quite scrambled up, with permanently low-status people temporarily elevated to high-status positions. Very young people found themselves in high positions.

Gradually technical problems were mastered and reduced to procedures and programs. Bureaupathic patterns became more pronounced. There were constant reorganizations, a growing volume of reports, increasing insistence upon clearance protocol, authority impressed for its own sake, not as a problem-solving device. Hierarchical dominance was pressed through a great variety of rituals—"control" boards, frequent staff meetings, calls to the "front office," progress reports, increasing insistence upon formal channels, etc.[5] These manifestations of authority were ritualistic because they were not related to winning the war, but to the "need for control." The organization product was not affected by them, because it was secured through an elaborate routine, of which no one comprehended more than a small part. Bureaupathic behavior occupied much more of the time of officials. They became kings' messengers after the kings were gone.[6]

Decision-Making Groups," *J. Abnorm. and Soc. Psychol.*, Vol. XLVIII (1953), pp. 231-8.

[5] See Victor A. Thompson: op. cit., Part Two.

[6] The technical problem military organizations must solve is winning a war. In peacetime, with no technical problem to solve, bureaupathic patterns are more pronounced. Arthur K. Davis says they live and survive in peacetime on ritual. "Bureaucratic Patterns in the Navy

10. *Bureautic Behavior*

The bureaucratic culture makes certain demands upon clients as well as upon organization employees. There are many people in our society who have not been able to adjust to these demands. To them bureaucracy is a curse. They see no good in it whatsoever, but view the demands of modern organization as "red tape." This kind of behavior is external to the organization, and is not simply a reaction to bureaupathology. Its source will be found within the critic himself, not within the organization. It is, in fact, a kind of social disease which we propose to call "bureausis."

Whereas the basic ingredient of bureaupathology is personal insecurity in authority positions, the basic ingredient of bureausis is immaturity, the dysfunctional persistence of childish behavior patterns. Before describing and analyzing the symptoms of bureauticism, let us briefly list those childish patterns which we believe to underlie this disease.

The child feels powerless and constantly fears abandonment by his parents. He does not feel that he can do anything by himself, but must depend upon others over whom he has no assured control. The child does not abstract well and so personalizes the world to make it comprehensible. He sees human agency in most events and imputes human motives to events, motives like his own. Thus, he projects himself into his environment.

The child cannot bind time; he cannot invest or cathect energy in future goals. The image of the object and the investment of energy occur together. He must have the object immediately; tomorrow he will have forgotten. The child has little skill in taking on the roles of others, in putting himself in someone else's place. He experiences himself directly and immediately and expects others to experience him in the

---

Officer Corps," *Social Forces,* Vol. XXVII (1948), pp. 143-53. He hypothesizes that "the effectiveness of military leaders tends to vary inversely with their exposure to a conventionally routinized military career." This study is reproduced in Merton, *et al.,* eds.: *Reader in Bureaucracy* (Glencoe, Illinois: The Free Press; 1952), pp. 380 ff.

same way. Consequently, to have to explain himself, especially to a parent, frequently makes him furious. If the parent were not so dense he would know the child as the child knows himself. On the other hand, the child never imagines a consciousness different from his own and so never really knows anybody but himself.

When the child is very small, he grows accustomed to receiving love without a price. Most very small children today are loved by their parents simply because they are there, not for what they do. Most parents gradually wean the child from this absolute security by making their love somewhat contingent upon performance and by withdrawing love for poor performance. In this way the child is gradually socialized and acquires a conscience. Many children, however, never have to pay much for their parents' love; they become "spoiled." They carry into adulthood the habit of receiving gratifications without a corresponding return or effort on their part.

In our discussion of the actual symptoms of bureausis, we will depend heavily upon Alvin Gouldner's short but suggestive study of the "red-tape" reaction.[7] Gouldner began his study with the very commonsensical, but nevertheless unusual assumption that when a person criticizes an organizational action or requirement as red tape, we should investigate the person so reacting as well as the organization.

As would be expected, Gouldner's respondents discussed their feelings about red tape in the language of efficiency, referring to things which were "unnecessary." However, efficiency, like its synonym, rationality, is a term which, though universal in form, is relative in content. The efficient or rational action is the one that gives the actor the most favorable ratio between accomplishments and costs, between its positively valued consequences and its negatively valued consequences. The efficient action, therefore, always promotes a system or ordering of values, never a single goal or end-in-view. People order their values differently, so that even if two people sought the same goal

---

[7] Alvin W. Gouldner: "Red Tape as a Social Problem," in Robert K. Merton, et al., eds.: op. cit., pp. 410 ff.

they might not agree as to which means for achieving it was most efficient or rational. Terms like efficient, rational, wasteful, or unnecessary, therefore, seem to refer to universal qualities of actions but actually hide personal preferences under these universalistic façades. Gouldner found a great differentiation of values behind the concept of "unnecessary." What was "unnecessary" to one person was not so to another.

The fact that someone feels requirements are unnecessary is certainly no reason to punish him by calling him "sick." People are entitled to their values and beliefs. If, however, a person's values and beliefs make it difficult for him to adjust to the kind of world he must live in, we are at least entitled to label them "dysfunctional." On the other hand, the innovator is also a person who is not completely adjusted to things as they are. Here, then, as in our discussion of bureaupathology, we are dealing with questions of degree. We wish to use our disease metaphor only for rather extreme cases of resistance to bureaucracy. There is a striking similarity between the reaction patterns of bureautics and certain behavior patterns of children, and so we have concluded that the bureautic syndrome is essentially a failure of maturation. It is important to remember, however, that immaturity, like insecurity, is a matter of degree.

From Gouldner's material, and from common observation, we can see that the bureautic resists interrogation and investigation as "unnecessary." They invade his privacy. Other people have no right to know these things about him —for example, his father's occupation (about which he may or may not be proud). Furthermore, they should not have to check up on *him*. He knows he is honest and his claim is valid, why don't they? The processing of his case shows he is dependent upon outside powers and processes beyond his control. It challenges his security and impugns his worth. He, as a person, is being weighed in the balance. Security patterns of childhood are being frustrated; a price is being charged for his satisfactions. The bureaucracy does not respond to him simply because he is *he*. Consequently, all the processing is unnecessary. "It's just a lot of red tape."

The bureautic has low powers of abstraction. He personalizes his world to make it comprehensible. Gouldner found that his critics of bureaucracy frequently preferred situations where "cash talked," or where relationships were personalized. The corner grocery store was a model; there was no red tape there. They could not understand complex, impersonal procedures and regarded them all as being "befuddled," "confused," and meaningless. This desire for simpler, more personalized relationships is often verbalized as a preference for "the good old days," but the only "good old days" which modern bureautics ever knew were the good old days of childhood.

By virtue of his need to personalize the world, the bureautic can rarely enter successfully into an impersonal, functional, or *bureaucratic*, relationship. The world is peopled only with friends and enemies; it does not have impartial, impersonal functionaries. The doctor, the postman, the service-station attendant, all must be taken into the bosom of the family. Only first names will do.

Bureautics fear the world beyond, the nonpersonalized world, and they fear bureaucracy because they cannot personalize it. They feel powerless in relation to it, on the "outside;" they feel alienated from the larger part of society. There are many things they are entitled to, but cannot get because this monstrous impersonal world does not respond to their desires. They crave the response to their needs that they used to get in childhood, an immediate and tender response from everyone. The bureautic is not satisfied with the limited number of situations in which he does have power, but wants to be the center of attraction *everywhere*. When this is denied, as it must be, he feels powerless and alienated.[8]

[8] Gouldner (op. cit.) suggests that an ideological group, the ultra-conservatives, is composed largely of such alienated people. The "good old days" of special privilege are passing. Bureaucracy is hostile to "amicism"—the pursuit of interests by means of personal contacts with strategically situated high-status social peers. This group has been important in developing the epithet "red tape." However, as we said above, as time goes by, the "good old days" must be interpreted as the "good old days" of childhood.

Because the bureautic cannot abstract and therefore personalizes the world, his frustrations must be the work of enemies. He tends to be suspicious of everything. The "unnecessary" requirements are a deliberate attempt to frustrate him or to deprive him of his rights. He is likely to believe that special privilege exempts others from these requirements and assures *their* satisfactions. "You have to have pull." He suspects that everyone in power has "pull," and that is how they got there. There is no point in working hard or being otherwise virtuous because "they" never reward merit. He projects his personal failings onto the "system," and his personal motives onto every one else. Since he rewards his friends and punishes his enemies, he suspects that the whole world operates on this principle. Consequently, he is likely to believe that the only successful approach to bureaucracy is through the personalized route of special favors and bribes or threats to "get them." He has no confidence in securing justice through an impersonal, abstract system of norms and routines, and he interprets justice as getting what is his by right. For him, "what is his by right" and what he wants are easily confused. Suspicion of others not only is a projection of his own motives, but it also builds up his ego. It is hard for him to believe that other people are so little concerned with him, so involved in their own problems, that they have neither the time nor the inclination to fabricate plots against him.

The bureautic is not skillful in taking on the roles of others. This lack of skill is part of the more general inability to abstract. He puts himself in another's place and therefore imputes malicious motives to other people, but he cannot put *another* in *his* place and therefore cannot imagine how others really feel. Because he cannot take on the role of the generalized other, he regards any checking of his claims as an unnecessary invasion of his privacy. He knows his claim is justified, his information honest and correct, and so of course he would not check himself. Therefore, why does the "other" check him? It is either unnecessary or malicious meddling. Of course, when others make claims on him, he will check them out carefully because they are "trying to put something over" on him. The fact that others require what is "unnecessary" can only be attributed to stupidity or maliciousness; in either case it is red tape. The bureautic's inability to abstract or generalize makes it impossible for him to understand why an exception cannot be made in his case. How could this one little exception possibly hurt anything? Refusal to grant the exception is bureaucratic officiousness, inconsiderateness, or disinterest. It is the ritualistic application of rules and regulations "whether they make sense or not."

The bureautic person probably has an underdeveloped power of investing energy in future objects. Gouldner's data suggest this. Waiting for gratification is therefore unusually painful and provokes the red-tape reaction. Of course, the dislike of waiting is particularly a matter of degree. No one likes it, but normally a person's ability to wait grows stronger as he matures. If this ability is underdeveloped in an adult, experiences with bureaucracy will be especially frustrating because, as we have shown, the large complex organization must normally move with a certain deliberateness. Perhaps the impact of the inability to defer gratifications must be assessed in connection with the other bureautic characteristics discussed above. If the waiting is "necessary," it is tolerable. If it is "unnecessary," it is intolerable; it is red tape. The question again becomes, what is "unnecessary"? The inability to defer gratifications provides emotional reinforcement for all of the frustrations of the bureautic in a bureaucratized world.

We have been discussing the bureautic as a client, but bureautics also become employees of bureaucratic organizations. Alternatives to this kind of employment are becoming fewer and fewer. Within the organization, the bureautic manifests the same suspiciousness of the motives of others. People are "out to get him." He feels that only those with "pull" get ahead. He cannot understand the reasons for many regulations and procedures, does not bother to familiarize himself with them, and constantly violates them. He will frequently refuse to keep required records or make required reports, often thereby creating vast confusion and enormous amounts of additional work for others. He insists on personalizing all relationships. To him the organization is a great battleground between his friends and him, on the one side, and "the rest," his enemies, on the other. In this battle, personal loyalties are all that count. He tends to lose sight of the organization as an instrument for accomplishing goals, as a structure of instrumental functions and relationships.

The bureautic employee is not likely to get into the hierarchy, and so may come to be regarded as a failure. Because of his inability to enter intelligently into abstract, complex, co-operative relationships, he tends to be pushed to one side, unless he has some unusual skill that the organization badly needs. He is often regarded as "queer." All of these facts add to his bitterness and increase his suspiciousness. He projects his failures onto the organization and the impersonal "others" who are his enemies. He feels he is surrounded by stupidity and maliciousness. He feels powerless and alienated from the organization.

In the preceding pages we have suggested that some adverse reactions to modern organizations stem from inadequacies in the reacting person rather than from inadequacies in these organizations. We realize that this subject is a delicate one and that people may honestly differ as to where the inadequacy resides in specific cases. Nevertheless, the fact remains that some people are uncomfortable with almost all aspects of modern organizations, while others work with them quite effectively. The former we have called bureautics, suggesting some failure in their maturation. We are aware that some people will argue that anyone who *can* adapt to modern bureaucracy should be called bureautic, and in one way it does not matter which group gets the name. However, there is the distinction of maturity and immaturity which will survive any semantic switching of names.

Of course, a well man shares many behaviors with a sick one. Who has not felt powerless before the large organization? It is true that, with a request, one is likely to be shunted from person to person; that he can find many who can say "no" but has difficulty finding the one who can say "yes." The reason for this fact, as we explained in a previous chapter, is that hierarchical institutions overstress the veto. A veto is final, but an approval frequently must go to a higher source, where it is again subject to a veto.

It is also undoubtedly true that modern organizations have many routines and requirements that really are unnecessary. Frequently people react to requirements as red tape simply because they do not know the reasons for them. The organization can remove this reaction by explaining the reasons for the requirements. In attempting to explain these reasons, officials sometimes find that there are no very good ones, and the requirements are changed. This sort of self-scrutiny to remove traditional deposits is part of the ethos of bureaucracy. It reflects the dominance of a spirit of rationalism brought into organizations by science and technology.

We have distinguished three kinds of behavior patterns which have often been conceptually confused. First are patterns characteristic of large, complex organizations based upon advanced specialization. These are *bureaucratic* patterns of behavior; *specialization* determines their nature.

A second kind consists essentially of exaggerations of bureaucratic behavior by insecure persons in hierarchical and nonhierarchical authority positions. These behaviors are oriented to personal needs rather than to organizational goals. They interfere with goal accomplishment and are, therefore, pathological from the standpoint of the organization. Consequently, we have called them *bureaupathic* behaviors; they arise from personal *insecurity*.

Finally, we have described a pattern of behavior which is a *reaction* to modern organizations by people (including both employees and clients) who are unable to adjust to the complexity, impersonality, and impartiality of these organizations. We have argued that the basis of this nonadjustive reaction is personal immaturity. We have called this pattern of behavior *bureautic*. Bureaucratic behavior is associated with specialization, bureaupathic behavior with personal insecurity, and bureautic behavior with personal immaturity.

CHAPTER 9

Co-operation

♣

1. *The Need for Co-operation*

According to Durkheim, the advance of the specialization of the individual coincides with the disappearance of the common conscience and with the decline of the "mechanical" solidarity which the common conscience produced. A new kind of solidarity becomes necessary to provide a basis for the moral regulation of society if normlessness or "anomie" is to be avoided. Conflict becomes less tolerable with growing interdependence. At the same time that specialization is destroying the common conscience, it creates the possibility of a new, "organic" solidarity based upon mutually recognized interdependence.

In order for this new solidarity to emerge, artificial obstacles to the true specialization of individuals must be eliminated. People must be allowed to develop according to their capacities and their tastes, and they must be rewarded according to their contributions. There must be equality of opportunity; there must be social justice.[1]

[1] If industrialism is not identical with specialization, it is at least ▲

In the modern period of specialization, the one desideratum that overshadows all others in importance is co-operation. The activities of specialists must be meshed together, and the predisposition to submit to this co-ordination is what we mean by co-operation. Consequently, the test of social institutions cannot be only their productivity. Also of importance is whether they promote co-operation. Organizational and managerial devices usually have the manifest function, or purpose, of production. They also have a latent function, an unplanned consequence, of affecting the co-operative system in some way, positively or negatively. The latent function must become manifest. The needs for products change, but the need for co-operation grows more intense. The ultimate test of organizational practices, therefore, must be their effect on the co-operative system. If man can solve the problem of co-operation, it becomes increasingly difficult to say that anything is impossible for him to accomplish.

The co-ordination required by a group of specialized individuals is no more than the orderly regulation of interdependence, the formal promulgation of interdependence. Organizations require, therefore, a legitimating mechanism, some device for distinguishing the official, or the "formal," from the unofficial. The hierarchical distribution of authority is such a device. Through this device the "official" position is defined; organizational legitimacy is conferred. Through the hierarchy, official communication flows. The official position and inquiries concerning it are transmitted through this channel. Choice between two or more positions all seeking official blessing is called decision making or conflict settlement. It seems to be true that only one official position can be tolerated; otherwise, the organization would pull apart. In this sense, all organizations are monistic. The term "an organization" or "the organization" implies this minimal or basic monism.

---

by-product of it. Industrialism is associated with the elimination of institutions which block social mobility, such as closed classes, special privileges, amicism, nepotism, sexual and racial discrimination, absolute monarchy, clericalism, slavery, serfdom, etc.

Co-operation implies an attitude toward co-ordination, which is the formalized regulation of interdependence. It is an attitude of agreement to the system of co-ordination, of willingness to be co-ordinated. These considerations raise to a position of central importance the question of how the system of co-ordination is put into effect. Weber's contention that it makes no difference appears, therefore, erroneous. Since the regulatory system must be consistent with the requirements of specialized interdependence, autocratic promulgation must be a *pro forma* matter of conferring legitimacy; otherwise the regulatory system threatens the co-operative system.

The regulatory system must be technically compatible with the system of interdependence if co-operation is to be preserved. It must also be compatible with the personal needs of the participants. As we have repeatedly said, organizations must satisfy some personal needs of their members as well as move toward some official goal. Devices for regulating interpersonal relations are probably rarely neutral. They have therapeutic or antitherapeutic effects; they increase or decrease tensions. Although there appears to be some evidence to the contrary, it seems likely that nonautocratic regulation is therapeutic, at least in a democratic culture. It is more likely to be consistent with the personal needs of participants. It is, consequently, more likely to promote co-operation than is autocratic regulation.[2]

With these preliminary considerations in mind, we can turn our attention to some basic problems of co-ordination in modern bureaucratic organizations. We will discuss three basic approaches to co-ordination: co-ordination through command, through group identifications, and through the mutually recognized interdependence of freely specialized individuals.

[2] See John W. Thibaut and Harold H. Kelley: *The Social Psychology of Groups* (New York: John Wiley & Sons, Inc.; 1959). Perhaps it would be better to say that nonarbitrary regulation is more likely to be therapeutic, and democratic processes are more likely to produce such regulation.

2. Co-ordination by Command

The monistic conception seeks co-ordination through a hierarchical structure of command authority. Since each person's behavior is considered to be determined by the commands of his superior, if every superior is able to give integrated, rationally consistent commands, the organization will automatically be a co-ordinated system of behavior.

Among other things, co-ordination through command requires a strong system of authority, a highly legitimated system. As authority weakens, punishments and rewards become ever more crucial as a part of the system of co-ordination. Subordinates must be coerced into doing what they no longer feel obligated to do. There accumulate unanticipated consequences at war with the requirements of co-ordination. Participation tends to be minimal. Spontaneity and initiative decline.[3] A larger and larger share of the organization's resources must be allocated to the administration of rewards and punishments with associated intelligence activities.

Punishment-centered administration appeals to immature and regressive tendencies in people, to fear, dependency, refusal to assume responsibility, escapism, etc.[4] It is

[3] Under the assumptions of co-ordination through command, initiative and spontaneity are theoretically unnecessary.

[4] See Harold J. Leavitt: *Managerial Psychology* (Chicago: University of Chicago Press; 1958), pp. 264-5; Cecil A. Gibb: "Leadership," in Gardner Lindzey, ed.: *Handbook of Social Psychology* (Reading, Massachusetts: Addison-Wesley Publishing Company, Inc.; 1954); David Krech and Richard S. Crutchfield: *Theory and Problems of Social Psychology* (New York: McGraw-Hill Book Co.; 1948); and Chris Argyris: "The Individual and Organization: Some Problems of Mutual Adjustment," *Admin. Sci. Q.*, Vol. II (1957), pp. 1-22, and "Understanding Human Behavior in Organizations: One Viewpoint," in Mason Haire, ed.: *Modern Organization Theory* (New York: John Wiley & Sons, Inc.; 1959). Argyris says, in effect, that modern bureaucratic (monistic) organization is incompatible with the healthy development of mature adults.

In a personal communication to Cecil Gibb, R. B. Cattell, the

based on essentially pessimistic assumptions about human motivation. The subordinate is pictured as a highly individualistic combination of laziness and greed.[5] Life is pictured as a harsh, competitive struggle of man against man. Resulting management practices depress co-operation, the willingness to be co-ordinated. The resulting order is monistic because it is autocratic. It issues from the right to command and is therefore likely to overlook the adequacy of, or the need for, the regulatory system because consent is irrelevant. Since the legitimating or authoritative, rather than the problem-solving or instrumental, aspect of the system of order is stressed, orders or commands tend to become ends in themselves rather than merely facilitative arrangements. Under such administration, resistance to commands becomes the occasion not for problem-solving analysis, but for punishment.[6]

Co-ordination through command assumes the monistic structure of influence, each person in the system being legitimately subject to influence only from the person above

---

psychologist, stated that autocratic leadership exploited primitive, regressive, and unconscious needs such as father dependence, vicarious satisfaction through identification, and superego projection instead of individual conscience. Gibb: op. cit., p. 909.

[5] H. B. Drury: *Scientific Management: A History and Criticism* (New York: Columbia University Press; 1921), p. 221. See also Frederick W. Taylor: *The Principles of Scientific Management* (New York: Harper & Brothers; 1911). Also Georges Friedman: *Industrial Psychology* (Glencoe, Illinois: The Free Press; 1955), p. 84. The latter points out that this view of worker motivation has long been prevalent. For a thorough demolition of this crude concept of worker motivation, see Moore: op. cit., pp. 170 ff., and pp. 259-60. For a good argument that modern theories of organization from Max Weber onward are impregnated with pessimism, see Gouldner: "Metaphysical Pathos and the Theory of Bureaucracy," *The Am. Polit. Sci. Rev.*, Vol. XLIX (June 1955), pp. 496-507.

[6] Alvin W. Gouldner: *Studies in Leadership: Leadership and Democratic Action* (New York: Harper & Brothers; 1950), ch. xi, refers to this approach as "punishment-centered bureaucracy" as opposed to "representative bureaucracy." In the latter, the system of order is merely an instrument to aid in achieving shared values and hence is based upon consent.

him in the hierarchy. Specialization has long outrun human ability to co-ordinate in this fashion. Not only is the person in the command position increasingly dependent upon subordinates for the interpretation of incoming data and the initiation of activities, but interdependencies far beyond command jurisdictions have developed. Consequently, most co-ordination is programmed, built into routines. It is this very routinization of activities that chiefly distinguishes bureaucracy from earlier charismatic forms. There result two conflicting systems of regulation, one based upon the necessities of technical interdependence, the other upon the rights and powers of hierarchical positions. One of the purposes of this book has been to show that these two systems are increasingly at war with one another.[7]

3. Co-ordination through Group Identification

Still a third regulatory system is found to be at work in the organization. In recent years, social scientists have pointed out the amazing extent to which individuals are regulated and co-ordinated by the informal groups of which they are members. Values and reality perceptions are shared by members of informal groups, and deviant tendencies are held in check by the informal activities of the group. It is not surprising that attempts are now being made to tap this truly enormous power over the individual as a device for obtaining co-ordinated action throughout the *formal* organ-

[7] Henri De Man said that the hierarchical system of production, or, as we would say, bureaucratic organization, is poisoned by the mingling of productive discipline and social subordination. *Joy in Work*, trans. Eden and Cedar Paul (London: George Allen and Unwin, Ltd.; 1929), pp. 200-4. Leavitt has pointed out that each working problem is actually a double problem, how to get the particular job done, and how to please the boss. (Op. cit., pp. 264-5.) Benjamin M. Selekman says there are "two sources of imposed co-operation, the one implicit in impersonal technology and the other explicit in personal shop authority. . . ." He traces conflict to this source. *Labor Relations and Human Relations* (New York: McGraw-Hill Book Co.; 1947), p. 222.

ization. If the individual can be attached to the organization by the same kind of ties which bind him to his informal working group, or if all such groups can be induced to move in a common direction, co-ordinated action can be obtained by the same force which keeps the informal group moving as an entity—shared values, attitudes, and perceptions of reality.

This group-identification approach to co-ordination recognizes the importance of co-operativeness, the willingness to be co-ordinated. It recognizes the failure of the old individualistic incentives. However, before the power of the subgroup can be used to reinforce formal organization effort, the values of the subgroup must be compatible with the official values of the organization.[8] Consequently, emphasis is placed on the sharing of goals and values throughout the organization.[9]

The organization seeks converts. Hard work is not enough.[1] Since neither the official values nor the product of most organizations can be very important to most of the people in them, conversion, to the extent it occurs, must be obtained by manipulation.[2] More often, we suspect, conversion does not occur but is simulated, resulting in a great deal of phony co-operativeness and hypocrisy.[3] It is hard to

[8] See Edward A. Shils: "Primary Groups in the American Army," in Robert K. Merton and Paul F. Lazarsfeld, eds.: *Continuities in Social Research: Studies in the Scope and Method of "The American Soldier"* (Glencoe, Illinois: The Free Press; 1950).

[9] Nearly all the modern, more "enlightened" approaches to organization stress the importance of sharing goals, if co-operation and co-ordination are to be achieved. For example, Selekman (op. cit., p. 223) says management must consciously create the sense of community among men at work because it does not arise spontaneously.

[1] As Whyte says, whereas the former boss wanted your sweat, the present one wants your soul as well. *The Organization Man* (Garden City, New York: Doubleday & Company, Inc.; 1957), p. 440.

[2] Manipulators want something for nothing. In free exchange, each side "manipulates" the other; each gets something he wants more for something he wants less; each prospers.

[3] Even in "total institutions" where the "management" control is much greater than in the ordinary bureaucratic organizations, for example, in mental hospitals or merchant ships, "conversion" is appar▶

understand the demand of the modern organization for the individual's soul as well as his good effort. Our contention is that this kind of behavior reflects growing insecurity in the authority system; it reflects a declining legitimacy.[4] It should be noted that the demand for total involvement increases as one mounts the hierarchy, until many individuals in high positions find that their community, religious, and even family life become simply aspects of their organizational duty.[5]

Although some individuals undoubtedly give considerable loyalty to their bread-and-butter organization, it is only one loyalty among many. If the organization becomes the only object of one's loyalty, then the organization becomes a totalitarian state. Most people probably give their first or primary loyalty to their primary groups—the family, the informal work group, etc. The sharing of values and reality perceptions throughout the larger organization is, therefore, an illusion. As we said above, it is a false loyalty.[6] More normally, the shared values and reality per-

---

ently more simulated than real, and most inmates keep their identities by "playing it cool." See Erving Goffman: "Characteristics of Total Institutions," in Maurice Stein, Arthur J. Vidich, and David Manning White, eds.: *Identity and Anxiety* (Glencoe, Illinois: The Free Press; 1960), pp. 449-79, especially pp. 462-3.

[4] It has often been pointed out that when the basic, legitimating values and beliefs of a system of authority come into doubt, overt proclamations of loyalty and adherence to these values and beliefs are vehemently demanded.

[5] See Whyte: op. cit., chs. xi, xii, and xiii. Note the organization's growing interference in the political beliefs and activities of its corporate personnel. "Corporations Make Politics Their Business," *Fortune* (December, 1959).

[6] It is interesting to watch the rapidly progressive deterioration of this loyalty at an organizational social affair. As noted in a previous chapter, with success defined as "moving up," most people must "fail." Resulting feelings of rejection can best be managed by failing to identify with the organization which rejected them. The difficulty of establishing a strong formal organization identification is underlined by the March and Simon listing of elements which promote such an identification. It will be noted that bureaucratic structure, and especially

ceptions extend only as far as the group of people who are in frequent communicative interaction—the informal working group or groups.

Co-ordination through group identification is co-ordination based upon the "common conscience," upon similarities of psychic content, and cannot, consequently, extend far enough to include all activities which need to be co-ordinated. The interdependencies arising from specialization extend much further than the face-to-face working group. The reliance upon group solidarity, therefore, is regressive —one might say a measure of desperation. It should be noted, furthermore, that to the extent that group identifications cannot be perfectly manipulated, their promotion involves some loss of control and is therefore self-defeating from the standpoint of the promoters.[7]

---

the rights of superiors, are hardly compatible with a high degree of organization identification. Their list is as follows:

1. Consensus as to means and ends
2. Lack of competition
3. Permissiveness with regard to personal goals or needs
4. A great amount of interaction
5. Great vertical mobility
6. General rather than close supervision
7. Employee-minded rather than production-oriented supervision
8. Participation in policy decisions

James G. March and Herbert A. Simon: *Organizations* (New York: John Wiley & Sons, Inc.; 1959), pp. 65 ff.

[7] See Philip Selznick: *TVA and the Grass Roots* (Berkeley: University of California Press; 1949). It is doubtful, for example, that participation can be extended without sharing power or influence. See Thompson: op. cit., ch. v. Thus, if participation is used as a control device, it may be self-defeating. Furthermore, the achievement of a high degree of organization identification may result in loss of control by encouraging the rationalization of behavior which deviates from organizational norms. "This good old organization wouldn't want me to do anything I didn't want to do." Many situations have been discovered where high output was associated with low morale. See a very strong quote from Rensis Likert on this point in Whyte: op. cit., p. 64. See also Morris S. Viteles: *Motivation and Morale in Industry* (New York: W. W. Norton & Co.; 1953), and A. H. Brayfield and W. H. Crockett: "Employee Attitudes and Employee Performance," *Psychol. Bulletin*, Vol. LII (1955), pp. 396-424.

4. Co-ordination and
Recognized Mutual Interdependence

From our analysis of co-ordination through command and through group identification, it would appear that some other basis for co-ordination is needed, is perhaps being slowly thrust upon us. It is hard to overlook the power of Durkheim's insight into this problem. Under advanced specialization, co-operativeness must depend upon recognized and accepted mutual interdependence. Since psychic similarities become attenuated with progressive differentiation, the common conscience is less and less available as a basis for interpersonal regulation.

Whereas group identification, on the one hand, is regressive and cannot in any case extend far enough to embrace all of those whose actions must be co-ordinated, the recognition of mutual interdependence, on the other hand, is consistent with personal maturity and is capable of providing as broad a basis for co-ordination as is technically needed.[8] Co-ordination based upon this mutual recognition of need cannot, of course, be arbitrarily imposed by authority. Although legitimating devices will still be required, they will be used to give official sanction to relations which are generally recognized to be technically necessary. Authority is necessary, but it must be disciplined by reason and reality.[9] In organizing, in dividing up the work and delegat-

---

[8] Jean Piaget says that the moral sense evolves from rule by others, or heteronomy, to rule by self, or autonomy. "The more complex the society, the more autonomous is the personality and the more important are the relations of co-operation between equal individuals." *The Moral Judgement of the Child*, trans. Marjorie Gabain (Glencoe, Illinois: The Free Press; 1948), p. 336. According to this conclusion of Piaget, co-ordination by command would be even more regressive than co-ordination by group identification. In fact, if Piaget is correct, the authoritarian structure of modern organization is not consistent with the maturation of the individual, as Chris Argyris has been arguing for some time.

[9] Leavitt points out that although authority is necessarily restrictive, it need not be frustrating. (Op. cit.) This point is essentially the

ing jurisdictions, authority must submit to the needs of specialization. With status and function for all, interdependencies will be acceptable, or at least tolerable, because the
necessity for them can be demonstrated. The official system
of regulation becomes a promulgation of a system of interdependence which already exists.

For such a system of co-ordination to work, there must
be a true equality of opportunity and a fair distribution of
rewards, especially the reward of recognition, of status or
deference. Individuals who are prevented from enjoying a
full measure of society's blessings because of man-made institutions can be expected to experience feelings of injustice as the legitimacy of those institutions declines. Here we
encounter, in addition to problems of social mobility, problems created by the hierarchical monopoly of "success."
The central problem of justice here is that the "success"
of one is dependent upon the "nonsuccess" of others.[1] "Success" is a function of a limited number of formal positions,
rather than of individual effort. "Success" is defined in

---

same as the one we have repeatedly made to the effect that the system
of regulation may be facilitative and tension-reducing if it is consistent
with specialization—if it formally recognizes a pre-existing technical
interdependence. See also Stephen A. Richardson: "Organizational Contrasts on British and American Ships," *Admin. Sci. Q.*, Vol. I (September, 1956).

[1] It seems likely that get-rich-quick goals are dependent upon a
large number of non-get-rich-quick goals. Likewise, success goals defined in terms of relative status or prestige are dependent upon success
goals defined in some other way, say, in terms of esteem within a
profession. It does not seem likely that organizations could survive if
all persons within them devoted themselves to the single-minded pursuit of improved status. Many people must adopt a different personal
objective and must consequently content themselves with getting the
job done. "Ambition" is thus seen to be a matter of cultural definition
and a useful ideological device. The many who do not "get ahead"
can be branded as unambitious, yet they are performing the work
which maintains the organization as an arena in which the competitive
struggle for status can continue to be waged. On this point, see Everett
C. Hughes: "Queries Concerning Industrial Society Growing out of
Study of Ethnic Relations in Industry," *Am. Sociol. Rev.*, Vol. XIV
(1949), pp. 218-20.

competitive terms of the status of a position, rather than in noncompetitive terms of esteem or of the able performance of a function. For esteem, one "competes" with himself; for status (i.e., "success") one competes with others.

Co-operation is the very antithesis of such competition. Since there is no way under the usual system to reward the idea man without threatening the competitive status position of others, he tends to be suppressed in our modern bureaucracies. In a regime based upon mutually recognized interdependence, however, with rewards appropriate thereto, he would be encouraged to make great contributions to group goals. Granting that change must be controlled, ideas could be qualified and directed by the demonstrable necessity of preserving the co-operative system, rather than suppressed because of the debatable need to protect the status system.

Specialist decisions must be group decisions if the solution of the problem at hand requires more than one kind of specialized competence. More and more organizational problems are of this kind. Many people deplore this decline of individual problem solving. However, we believe that problem solving by groups should generally be superior to individual problem solving, and particularly if the group is not formally structured by means of superior-subordinate role relationships. The greater effectiveness of group decision is not always realized in the formally structured group, however. As we pointed out in chapter five above, ideas do not stand on their merits alone in modern organizations, but must always be considered from the point of view of their impact on competitive personal goals of "success" as well. Participants at an organizational conference do not put all of their cards on the table; they say one thing and mean another. At one and the same time there is open and hidden decision making going on, and open and hidden communication. What appears to be a frank, open, rational, group problem-solving process is very often actually a bargaining or political process. The outcome is likely to be determined by power, even though on the surface it seems to be a result of rational analysis. What appears to be consensus at the end of the meeting is just as likely to be a smiling acknowledgment of victory on one side, and of defeat on the other.

5. *The Approach of Modern Management*

Essentially, modern management combines the group-identification approach and that of the individualistic command, despite the fact that in actual practice the two are basically incompatible. The group-identification approach is manifested by an emphasis on teams, teamwork, and group decision; upon the attempt to achieve organization-wide loyalties; upon morale building, and the employment of sociologists and psychologists to build "human relations" into the work situation; and upon the training of supervisors in group leadership and communication.

Chief reliance, however, is still placed upon the command power of the superior, backed up by an incentive system which appeals to a presumed universal desire to "get ahead" of others. Although changes are occurring, it would seem that the incentive system of modern management is still largely a matter of enforced individual competition. Piecework, bonuses, incentive awards, efficiency ratings, promotions, prizes, commendations—all stress individual competition, with the supervisor as the principal arbiter. He can withhold rewards; he can reprimand and secure dismissal. His is the power to punish. In the absence of a "common conscience," the act of inflicting punishment tends to become an act of sheer power, producing not cohesion but an adult-child relationship which reflects the immaturity of mankind. It obscures the fact that the superior is himself a member of the group and subject to obligations and loyalties deriving from such membership. He often finds himself in an intolerable position between two sets of conflicting demands.

If the incentive system of enforced individual competition were effective, so that each individual in the organization constantly acted in a way that would promote his own goals regardless of the effects this would have on the personal goals of his colleagues, there would be no cohesive working groups in modern organizations. These powerful sources of energy and motivation would be lost. Individualistic incentives can rarely lift behavior out of the ordinary. Heroic behavior is group-inspired behavior. Furthermore, it is doubtful that individual behavior can be successfully regulated without considerable assistance from group processes. Without groups, the organization would be, in truth, a jungle. Since modern management leans so heavily for incentives upon enforced individual competition, we are forced to come to the harsh conclusion that the successes of modern organizations derive to a considerable extent from the failures of their official incentive systems.[2]

The punishment-centered incentive system, pregnant as it is with unanticipated consequences, results ultimately in loss of control, of influence, and therefore of co-ordination. Particularly noticeable in this respect is what Robert Merton has called the "self-fulfilling prophecy."[3] For example, close, strict, and specific supervision attacks group cohesion and communication, encourages stratification which further blocks communication, and depresses initiative, spontaneity, and co-operativeness.[4] In other words, it creates the conditions

[2] Leavitt points out that enforced interpersonal competition is harmful to productivity as well as to solidarity unless (1) the jobs involved are technically independent of one another, (2) objective performance standards are available, and (3) success for one person does not mean failure to another. Obviously these conditions rarely prevail. (Op. cit., pp. 259-60.) He says that group reward systems, like profit sharing, have proved best in terms of productivity but are little used because they batter down hierarchical prerogatives and secrecy. (Ibid., p. 182.) As to the superior's power over such personal goals as promotion, he says that World War II experience demonstrated that sociometric ratings ("buddy" ratings) were a more valid basis for promotion but are not used because, again, they attack hierarchical rights. Ibid., pp. 95, 105.

[3] Robert K. Merton: *Social Theory and Social Structure* (Glencoe, Illinois: The Free Press; 1957), ch. xi.

[4] See Kurt Lewin: *Resolving Social Conflicts* (New York: Harper & Brothers; 1948). See also L. Coch and J. R. P. French, Jr.: "Overcoming Resistance to Change," *Human Relations*, Vol. I (1948), pp.

which seem to justify its use.[5] Managements then complain that modern employees will not think, use their imagination, or take responsibility, with the result that unusual, or charismatic, persons who can and will do these things must be found to supervise them.[6] Since such persons are allegedly scarce, great privileges must be given them. Such is the "self-fulfilling prophecy," which helps explain the circu-

---

512-32. See also D. McGregor: "Conditions of Effective Leadership in the Industrial Organization," *J. Consulting Psychol.*, Vol. VIII (1944), pp. 55-63. See also R. Lippitt and R. K. White: "The Social Climate of Children's Groups," in R. G. Barker, J. S. Kounin, and H. F. Wright, eds.: *Child Behavior and Development* (New York: McGraw-Hill Book Co.; 1943), pp. 485-508. Leavitt has pointed out that command, being one-way, is not communication at all, but that it protects the superior and can hide incompetence. Ibid., pp. 124-6.

[5] See Gouldner: *Patterns of Industrial Bureaucracy* (Glencoe, Illinois: The Free Press; 1954), pp. 159-80; and Chris Argyris: op. cit. This circularity is reinforced by the status system. The deference and unusual treatment given the superior may turn his head, causing him to believe he is a superior person and that for the good of all should engage in close and autocratic supervision.

The uncritical acceptance of the superiority of the superior is rather widespread and is in fact part of the ideological underpinning of bureaucratic authority and status. One interesting variation on this charismatic theme is the suggestion that the superior should use his authority (i.e., supervise) in a clinical fashion as a means to subordinates' goals and needs rather than as a threat thereto. See Leavitt: op. cit., ch. xii. See also Jack R. Ewalt: *Mental Health Administration* (Springfield, Illinois: Charles C. Thomas, Publisher; 1956), pp. 28-9. See also Paul Pigors and Charles A. Meyers: *Personnel Administration*, 3rd ed. (New York: McGraw-Hill Book Co.; 1956), ch. v. See also B. M. Selekman: op. cit., Part Three.

[6] See H. B. Drury: op. cit., p. 221; also Henry Ford: *My Life and Work* (Garden City, New York: Doubleday and Co.; 1922), p. 103. See Friedman's comment on these criticisms of modern workers. (Ibid., pp. 357, 153-4.) Since the monistic system defines the superior as the responsible person, it follows, again by definition, that subordinates are not responsible. Here again the many uses of the term make it a very handy ideological device. Furthermore, if a subordinate is not treated as a responsible adult, it is hardly possible for him to behave as one—another example of the circularity of the "bureaucratic" pattern, its self-fulfilling, self-rewarding nature.

larity which many theories of bureaucracy find in "bureaucratic" behavior.[7]

6. Rationalizing Modern Management

The approach to co-ordination through command is rooted
in the culture. It cannot be a technically rationalized part of
organization, because it reflects culturally defined rights of
hierarchical roles and is in fact the chief obstacle to further
technical rationalization, to the regulation of behavior on
the basis of recognized and accepted mutual interdependence.[8] Among the hierarchical rights particularly important in
this respect is the right to deference according to the status
system. Involved as it is with our system of distributive justice, the status system is especially resistant to change and
particularly to any further technical rationalizations attack-
ing it. Since "success" is defined as improved "scalar" status,[9]

[7] We have argued that personal insecurity is also involved in this
circular behavior; that, for example, close supervision satisfies the personal need for control, rather than the organizational need for co-
ordinated successful actions.

[8] See Henri De Man: op. cit., pp. 204-6. He points out that this
approach, when rooted in the culture, can survive even a revolution
in property relations, as it has in Russia. See also Carl Dreyfuss on the
functionality of prestige ranking in industry, in Merton, et al., eds.:
Reader in Bureaucracy (Glencoe, Illinois: The Free Press; 1952), pp.
258-64. See also Victor A. Thompson: The Regulatory Process in OPA
Rationing (New York: King's Crown Press; 1950), pp. 255 ff.

[9] Barnard uses this term for hierarchical status as opposed to
occupational status. "Functions and Pathology of Status Systems in
Formal Organizations," in William Foote Whyte, ed.: Industry and
Society (New York: McGraw-Hill Book Co.; 1946).
    Resistance to modification of hierarchical roles is not merely a
result of the status they command. Hierarchical positions provide incumbents with the ability to manipulate the organization for personal
goals, and therefore these positions become highly prized as ends in
themselves (rather than simply as means to organizational goals). A
competitive and more or less vicious struggle for these positions inevitably ensues. See Philip Selznick: "An Approach to A Theory of
Bureaucracy," op. cit. See also Lyman Bryson: "Notes on A Theory
of Advice," Polit. Sci. Q., Vol. LXVI (1951), pp. 321-9.

and since everyone must be given a chance at it, hierarchical positions cannot be restricted to persons who have been specially trained for them, and "management" cannot be rationalized. It must remain mysterious and charismatic, a matter more of rights and prerogatives than of specialized abilities.[1]

If they were stripped of exaggerated deference and disciplined by technical requirements, authority roles in modern organizations would become functional parts of an interdependent enterprise, like the quarterback on a football team or the coxswain on a rowing team. Activities performed in these roles would become subject to the same kind of instrumental questioning and modification as other activities in the organization. But under the romantic protection of the status system, such questioning becomes nothing less than *lèse majesté*, defined in our dictionary as an "offense against a ruler's dignity."

7. *Some Suggestions for Reform*

Social scientists are tempted to regard institutions as beyond man's rational powers of control. So regarding them gives the social scientist a solid subject matter, impervious to human wish, even as the physicist has. Thus, his claims acquire more credibility, his recommendations more legitimacy; and he himself acquires respectability. Institutions have been originated and changed, however, by conscious intelligence. We can, therefore, hardly escape making a few recommendations for institutional change. The great difficulty in engineering institutional change is in finding what John R. Commons called the "limiting factors"—important elements in the situation which can practically be altered by man's conscious efforts. Frontal attacks upon institutions are usually not feasible. What kinds of changes are needed should be clear enough from the previous analysis. Our few

---

[1] Recurring proposals for a specially trained administrative corps would have more chance of acceptance if hierarchy were not the only road to "success" and hence had to be left, at least theoretically, open to all.

suggestions in the following pages are intended merely as examples.

In the first place, it might be wise to give most persons in supervisory positions some specific instrumental functions in addition to the exercise of authority, such as the factory foreman and the college-department chairman have. Not only would this practice keep the supervisor so busy that he would be forced to forego close supervision; but it would keep him also in touch with the technical realities and the interdependencies of the organization.[2] With an important technical function, he could be expected to minimize concern with prerogative and protocol.

Secondly, a beginning might be made in the redefinition of "success" if organizations were to establish two equal salary scales, one for specialists and one for the hierarchy. Many persons would then feel that they could "get ahead" by earning esteem rather than by acquiring status. Some of the enormous waste of our country's technical and professional skill might thereby be avoided.[3] It is noteworthy

[2] It has also been suggested that increasing the number of subordinates would make it more difficult for a superior to engage in close supervision. Among many others, William F. Whyte has made this suggestion in a paper presented to the American Sociological Society at its meeting in 1956: "On the Evolution of Industrial Sociology." See Argyris: op. cit. This approach stresses the values of the rake type of organization which, in addition to repressing close supervision, reduces the number of hierarchical levels, hence status ranks. The rake type should reduce the supervisory salary bill, not only because the number of supervisors is reduced, but also because hierarchical salaries are to some extent an attempt to symbolize the system of status ranking. Thus, an organization with many hierarchical layers will probably have a very high salary at the top. See Wilbert E. Moore: *Industrial Relations and the Social Order*, rev. ed. (New York: The Macmillan Co.; 1951), p. 125. The "science" of position classification reaches the same result. Jobs are classified according to duties and responsibility. Since, according to monistic definitions, responsibility increases rapidly as we go up the hierarchy, position classification can tolerate very high salaries in the upper reaches of the hierarchy.

[3] We wonder whether our competition with Russia is not going to force some such practice upon us. Russia rewards her technical and professional specialists well enough to keep most of them in their spe-

that in organizations where the success of the organization itself is obviously dependent upon esteem won by its functional specialists, as in sports or other entertainment fields, such a double salary scale exists. Some academic departments are "managed" by "executive officers" from lower ranks rather than by "chairmen" from the upper ranks. Such a dual salary schedule would occasionally result in a situation (demolishing to status!) where the superior earns less than the subordinate.

Thirdly, the division of labor in each organization should be re-examined to bring it into line with the needs of specialization. Wherever machine technology allows, the microdivision of labor should be ended. No longer should we throw a large part of the man away. Labor should be upgraded as fast as possible.[4] This process is now going on at an increasingly rapid rate as automation, completing the promise of the industrial revolution, creates machines which no longer require bits and pieces of men to complete them.

Specialist interdependencies created by acts of authority rather than by the advance of specialization should

---

cialty. An autocratic political system, less dependent upon winning popular consent than is a democratic system, is more dependent upon technical and professional prowess and hence must keep its technical and professional people reasonably happy.

[4] Restraints to specialization, to the achievement of function and status for all, should be eliminated. Thus, such alleged practices as union resistance to the upgrading of Negro labor should cease. Although many have held that the microdivision of labor was compelled by advancing technology (see, for example, Talcott Parsons: *The Social System* [Glencoe, Illinois: The Free Press; 1951], pp. 507-8), this view confuses cause and effect. The desire to discipline industrial labor *informed* advancing technology. See Carl Dreyfuss: *Occupation and Ideology of the Salaried Employee,* trans. Ernest E. Warbling (New York: Columbia University Press; 1938), pp. 75 and 77, and sources cited above in ch. iii. Peter Drucker has shown how wartime labor shortages forced the grouping of minute activities into more elaborate complexes so that unskilled workers did the job of skilled workers and did it as well as it had been done before. *Concept of the Corporation* (New York: The John Day Co.; 1946), pp. 183-4. The point is that technology, as such, can develop in many directions as long as it stays within the bounds of basic scientific knowledge.

be abolished.[5] Necessary interdependencies can themselves be hard to tolerate, but unnecessary ones are intolerable. In this connection it should be remembered that specialty depends upon an existing body of technique or knowledge which the individual masters by training and practice. If such a body of knowledge or technique does not exist, naming someone a specialist in such technique or knowledge does not make him one. True specialties cannot be created by acts of authority, but only by practice. Copying a "function" from other organizations, therefore, does not create a function if it did not exist in the first place. Although we are just beginning to develop a respectable body of organization theory, there have been "organization experts" in organizations for years. We recommend, therefore, that all "staff specialties" be re-evaluated and that all of those lacking an existing and substantial body of knowledge or technique be eliminated. We are saying, in effect, that there should be decentralization wherever centralization cannot be shown to be necessary.

Finally, all organizational processes and arrangements should have as a manifest purpose the furthering of co-operation. It must, however, be co-operation based upon the mutual recognition and acceptance of interdependence, which is the only possible foundation. Such mutual recognition, in turn, will depend upon the achievement of status and function for all. Then men will become adults, and the grown-up kindergartens through which we now conduct our affairs will pass unregretted from the scene.

[5] Here we do not refer to jurisdictions created for control purposes which may be quite justified, such as position classification to achieve equal pay for equal work, but to delegations resulting from power plays, from managerial esthetic needs for uniformity, etc.

INDEX